The Five Elements of Professional Networking

ENDORSEMENTS

"An excellent primer with specific networking techniques for both the early and senior careerist. Chris recognizes the difference between 'drop-in' networking and developing a true, long-lasting relationship. He understands the value of personal connection as a vital element for long-term success. Much can be learned from Chris as he shares in a very personal and genuine way. He writes from experience and success, offering techniques to reference throughout your career."

Gary Fybel, Former Chief Executive, Scripps Memorial Hospital La Jolla

"As a so-called 'social introvert' whose life and career has been blessed by both long-term and new friendships, I can vouch for the validity and value of Chris Lee's systematic framework. It's so true that casual conversations often build the sense of community and belonging to a broader society. *The Five Elements of Professional Networking* provides a clear path to knowing others and being known."

Ken Perez, President, ScriptPro

"Chris is an effortless relationship-builder—genuine, consistent, and valuable. In this book, he has transformed the traditionally stuffy topic of 'networking' into something rewarding, accessible, and possibly even fun. With both real-life examples and play-by-play templates, he gives you a practical how-to guide while also laying out the human elements of relationship-building. Whether you're hoping to expand your professional horizons or just become better at relating to others, I'm sure you'll enjoy learning from him as much as I have."

Geri Kirilova, Managing Partner, Laconia Capital Group

"As a professor and program director at UCLA, my network has allowed me to build collaborations, recruit guest speakers, and stay informed of trends. *The Five Elements of Professional Networking* provides valuable guidance by demystifying the process of building relationships. Chris Lee draws from years of observation, offering practical insights that transcend typical clichés. He introduces a framework that anyone can adapt to their own personality and career stage."

Laura Erskine, Professor and Program Director, UCLA Fielding School of Public Health

"Chris Lee's approach to networking is authentic, thoughtful, and refreshingly down-to-earth. In this value-packed book, he digs into five key elements of networking that demystify relationship building. I found myself highlighting new ideas, memorable quotes, and practical tips in each chapter. Chris' approach is not just about climbing the career ladder but about living a meaningful and fulfilling life."

Jonathan Liu, MD, FACP, Principal, Health Strategy, Amazon

"*The Five Elements of Professional Networking* is an invaluable guide for building authentic, meaningful connections. Christopher K. Lee, a master of interpersonal skills, has taught me so much about the power of listening. As he wisely says, 'Listening well makes people feel valued,' and this book is filled with insights on how to engage with curiosity and create genuine relationships."

Bob Baker, VP of Engineering, Stax Payments

"As someone who has researched networking as an essential part of my job, I applaud Christopher Lee for presenting a fresh framework for networking. Rather than simply tactical advice, which often borders on manipulation, Chris provides a grounding in values as well as attention to effectiveness."

Mark Washington, National Director of MBA Ministry, InterVarsity Christian Fellowship

"*The Five Elements of Professional Networking* is an essential guide for building lasting professional relationships. With a clear and actionable framework, Chris Lee breaks down the art of networking into practical steps. Whether you're a student, entrepreneur, or executive, this book provides the tools to grow your network with authenticity and impact."

John Bradley Jackson, Director, CSUF Center for Entrepreneurship

"Networking is more than just meeting people—it's about building real relationships that create opportunities. *The Five Elements of Professional Networking* offers a clear and practical approach to making meaningful connections. As someone who works with entrepreneurs, I see firsthand how strong communication and credibility can open doors. This book is a valuable resource."

Ryan Foland, Director, UCI ANTrepreneur Center

"Networking is one of the most valuable yet misunderstood skills in business. *The Five Elements of Professional Networking* breaks it down into a framework that anyone can apply. Chris provides insightful strategies on building relationships with authenticity and purpose. Whether you're an entrepreneur, investor, or professional, this book is a must-read."

JC Ruffalo, Venture Partner, Cove Fund

"Chris is THE master networker. He is so good and natural that you do not even realize that he has a framework behind it until he actually shows it to you! And this is exactly how we met—Chris helped us secure our largest investment to date!"

Eric Alvarez, Founder and CEO, Grapefruit Health

"Career advancement often hinges on whom you know and how effectively you can collaborate. As the founder and CEO of a high-growth startup, I've witnessed how nurturing meaningful connections can open doors and shape one's professional trajectory. *The Five Elements of Professional Networking* delivers a practical framework that encourages personal reflection and growth. If you're serious about building a network that stands the test of time, Chris's insights are invaluable. I highly recommend!"

Shrey Kapoor, MD, Founder and CEO, MedSetGo

"Networking has been a cornerstone of my career. I've seen how the right connections can open doors. Chris Lee stands out not just as someone who knows how to network, but as someone who values relationships. If you want to get better at building connections, this book is a great guide."

Reza Hessamian, Manager, Healthcare M&A Advisory, PwC

"My career growth has always been driven by the people I've met and the relationships I've cultivated. Chris' work as a mentor and leader has shown me how much he cares about helping others succeed. *The Five Elements of Professional Networking* reflects that same thoughtfulness and provides practical advice for anyone looking to grow their professional network."

Andrew Nguyen, Product Manager, Kaiser Permanente

"I've seen firsthand how meaningful connections can open doors, create opportunities, and shape the future. Throughout my own journey in healthcare leadership, networking has been essential to influencing without authority, driving initiatives forward, and fostering collaboration. Chris' insights provide a practical framework that has the power to transform careers."

Kyle Underwood, Program Manager, Cleveland Clinic

"Christopher is grounded and purposeful in the way networking is done. He has helped me gain perspectives about my career in ways I had not envisioned. *The Five Elements of Professional Networking* will help you develop more meaningful relationships and realize your full potential."

Maryam Zeineddine, Project Manager, University of Southern California

"As an international student and a natural introvert, networking always felt like a challenge. No one ever truly teaches you how to do it, so I had my own misconceptions. This book completely changed my perspective. While it offers a clear and actionable framework for networking, it also serves as a deeper reflection on how we engage with people in our lives. I only wish I had read this book much earlier."

Ken Kobayashi, MD, Cardiologist and MBA Candidate, Columbia Business School

"As a student researcher who interacts with professors and colleagues across disciplines, I know that networking is crucial in today's ever-evolving professional world. I highly recommend *The Five Elements of Professional Networking* to anyone seeking to enhance their relationships and professional success."

Adriana Mares, MD Candidate, Yale School of Medicine

The FIVE ELEMENTS OF PROFESSIONAL NETWORKING

Building Blocks For Genuine Relationships And Successful Careers

CHRISTOPHER K. LEE

NEW YORK
LONDON • NASHVILLE • MELBOURNE • VANCOUVER • BOSTON

THE FIVE ELEMENTS OF PROFESSIONAL NETWORKING

Building blocks for genuine relationships and successful careers

© 2025 Christopher K. Lee

All rights reserved. No portion of this book may be reproduced, stored in a retrieval system, or transmitted in any form or by any means—electronic, mechanical, photocopy, recording, scanning, or other—except for brief quotations in critical reviews or articles, without the prior written permission of the publisher.

Published in New York, New York, by Morgan James Publishing. Morgan James is a trademark of Morgan James, LLC. www.MorganJamesPublishing.com

Proudly distributed by Publishers Group West®

Morgan James BOGO™

A **FREE** ebook edition is available for you or a friend with the purchase of this print book.

CLEARLY SIGN YOUR NAME ABOVE

Instructions to claim your free ebook edition:
1. Visit MorganJamesBOGO.com
2. Sign your name CLEARLY in the space above
3. Complete the form and submit a photo of this entire page
4. You or your friend can download the ebook to your preferred device

ISBN 9781636987095 paperback
ISBN 9781636987101 ebook
Library of Congress Control Number: 2025933678

Cover Design by:
Ale Urquide

Interior Design by:
Chris Treccani
www.3dogcreative.net

Morgan James PUBLISHING **Builds** with... **Habitat for Humanity** Peninsula and Greater Williamsburg

Morgan James is a proud partner of Habitat for Humanity Peninsula and Greater Williamsburg. Partners in building since 2006.

Get involved today! Visit: www.morgan-james-publishing.com/giving-back

Contents

Foreword .... *Xiii*
Preface .... *Xvii*
Introduction .... *Xxi*

Element 1:   Value 1
Element 2:   Initiative 27
Element 3:   Consistency 57
Element 4:   Relatability..................................85
Element 5:   Credibility 113

Conclusion *139*
Acknowledgments *151*
About The Author *155*
References *157*

FOREWORD

If you're like me early in my career—or like more than 4,500 people I've trained in career development over the past 15 years—you probably hear the word "networking" and immediately break into a cold sweat: "What do I do, just hand out business cards, right?"

That's the visual most people have. They picture a high-powered business mogul working the room at a networking event, slinging business cards like a Vegas blackjack dealer, shaking hands with the enthusiasm of a politician on election day, and dropping industry jargon like a TED Talk speaker.

That was my thought process as I sought to leave my first career—emergency medical services (EMS)—and transition into the world of politics. I quickly realized something: In politics, in business, in education, and even in your personal life, *networking is everything*.

But here's the kicker: I had no clue how to do it. I didn't have a networking guru showing me the ropes. Nope. I had to learn the hard way. Through trial and error. Lots and lots of errors.

There were times I showed up to events and just sat in the corner, eyes darting around the room wondering when someone would approach me. Then there were times I completely blanked on a name mid-conversation: "Hey... you!" (Spoiler: That is not a recommended networking strategy.)

Thankfully, by virtue of you holding this book, *you* are already ahead of the game.

The Five Elements of Professional Networking is a must-read for anyone looking to slay the dragon of professional networking. It provides a straightforward, actionable framework for building and sustaining relationships based on five core elements: value, initiative, consistency, relatability, and credibility. These aren't just buzzwords—these are the secret ingredients to transforming connections into real, lasting relationships that can open doors, create opportunities, and elevate your career.

And who better to teach you than Chris Lee?

I've had the pleasure of knowing Chris for many years. I've watched him grow from a shy undergraduate student to the world-class networking guru I wish I had when I started my professional journey. Chris doesn't just "do" networking. He lives it. And not in that slick, gimmicky, transactional way that makes you feel like you're being sized up for a business deal. No, Chris understands that networking isn't about collecting contacts—it's about building trust, creating value, and showing up for people in ways that make them want to show up for you.

I've watched Chris in action. He's the kind of person who doesn't just remember your name and that one obscure hobby you mentioned in passing six months ago. He doesn't just meet people—he connects with them, understands them, and seeks out meaningful opportunities for collaboration. And that's exactly what this book is going to teach you how to do.

Why does this matter? The ability to effectively build a strong network can mean the difference between a mediocre career, hindered by limited access to opportunities, and a stellar career, built on relationships with a coalition of allies actively looking for ways to help you succeed.

And if you're thinking, "But I'm an introvert. Networking isn't for me," don't worry—Chris has got you covered. This book isn't about forcing yourself into uncomfortable situations or pretending to be someone you're not. It's about learning how to be strategic, authentic, and intentional in how you build relationships—whether you're a student trying to land your first job, a seasoned professional looking to grow your influence, or a neighbor trying to rally support to finally get that pothole on your street filled.

At the end of the day, networking isn't about what you know—it's about whom you know. And more importantly, who knows the *authentic you*.

Looking back on my own career, I can say with absolute certainty that networking has played a defining role in every major opportunity I've had. When I first started in EMS, my focus was on patient care, not professional networking. But as I transitioned into health policy, and then healthcare management and leadership, I learned that relationships were the real currency of career advancement.

Networking opened doors I didn't even know existed. It connected me with mentors who guided my path, peers who challenged me to grow, and decision-makers who saw potential in me that I hadn't yet recognized in myself. Without those relationships, I wouldn't have had the chance to work on groundbreaking public health and workforce development initiatives; lead policy and advocacy efforts at a major academic medical center; or help a hospital system navigate the existential challenges of the COVID-19 pandemic as a C-suite executive.

And let's be clear—none of this happened because I was the smartest person in the room. It happened because I showed up.

Because I built thoughtful relationships with intention. Because I learned the value of consistency, credibility, and bringing something meaningful to the table.

Networking isn't just about climbing the corporate ladder—it's about making an impact. It's about creating alliances that lead to transformative initiatives, forming coalitions that tackle complex problems, and becoming a trusted, influential voice in your field. It's the reason I've been able to develop award-winning public relations and advocacy programs, secure funding for vital community health initiatives, and influence policy at every level of government.

So whether you're just starting out or looking to take your career to the next level, let *The Five Elements of Professional Networking* be your guide. The insights Chris shares will save you years of trial and error and give you a roadmap to building the kind of relationships that create real opportunities.

Now go forth and make some connections. And maybe—just maybe—remember people's names better than I did.

Aaron J. Byzak
Strategic Public Affairs Consultant
Four-time Emmy Award winner

PREFACE

We live in a world of constant change. In recent years, we've witnessed scientific breakthroughs, technological disruptions, sociopolitical upheavals, and cultural paradigm shifts. Some changes have been positive; others, not so much. Many would've been unimaginable just a decade ago.

Despite all these changes, one truth stays timeless: We all need other people.

We lead and manage employees. We follow and emulate mentors. We support and work alongside colleagues. We walk through life's joys and sorrows, highs and lows, with friends.

Relationships are an integral part of success, not just a means to achieve it. A winner with no friends is a loser. Someone who doesn't treat people right is not successful, regardless of how wealthy, skillful, or accomplished he may be. Likewise, a good business is measured not only in financial returns. As a prominent investor says, "Take care of the people, the products, and the profits—in that order."[1]

So how do you meet the right people? How do you foster positive, trusting relationships? How do you get started? For many people, the thought of networking can feel "like staring at a blank page."[2]

Blank pages are daunting. Without guidance or direction, it's hard to know where to begin. What is the prompt? What are the common styles and techniques? A good assignment has a clear problem, defined metrics, and expected deliverables. A well-designed game has specific objectives, transparent rules, and balanced mechanics. Networking, in large part, does not. It's what you make of it.

Yet blank pages can also feel liberating. In this book, I will help you see the possibilities. I will guide you to figure out your goals and find your approach. I will teach you all I know about networking.

Whom is this book for?
This book is for those who want to grow personally and professionally. Who seek to establish, advance, or transition their careers. Who recognize that relationships are key to achieving their goals.

I'm writing for college students and seasoned professionals alike. At first, I thought the topic would appeal mostly to early careerists. But after one speaking engagement, a co-presenter contacted me to ask about networking. Having been a therapist for 30 years, he wanted to transition into executive coaching. So he sought my advice on building relationships with corporate decision makers. I've met many people like him. They possess the technical skills and subject matter expertise in their fields. What they need are the social skills and mindset to achieve their career aspirations.

I'm writing for quiet introverts as well as social butterflies. I don't believe that introverts must act like extroverts to get ahead. Yes, growth requires leaving our comfort zones, and certain behaviors are favored in our society. But if you overextend and pretend to be someone you're not, you'll appear less genuine and less trustworthy. Social psychologist Amy Cuddy calls this disconnect "asynchrony."[3] We want to avoid that. Two of my early mentors were hospital CEOs. Their schedules were full of meetings and public appearances. They were adept at dealing with people. Yet both described themselves as introverts. Networking looked different for them than it did for extroverted leaders.

I'm writing for those who have been underestimated and overlooked, who have more to offer and just need a chance to prove it. I see you. I've walked in your shoes. A college professor refused to support me for clinical psychology PhD programs; she said I wasn't good at people skills. Perhaps she was right. But fast forward 10 years, friends come to me for advice on relationships. Colleagues seek my guidance on sensitive situations. One boss said that I have high EQ and wished she could replicate it across the company. Another wrote in a performance review: "Chris is excellent at networking and cultivating relationships." Likewise, don't write yourself off; your story is still being written.

Whether you're an employee or an entrepreneur, a student or an executive, good relationships form the foundation of success. This has been and will always be. That is why I'm writing this book.

I present to you *The Five Elements of Professional Networking* as the resource I wish I had.

INTRODUCTION

In the business world, few ideas are as popular yet misunderstood as professional networking.

Whether you have decades of experience or are now entering the workforce, you've likely heard that you should network with others. But ask 10 people what they mean, and you may receive 10 different answers. People use the same terms to mean different things. They use different terms interchangeably. And their views on how and why to network may conflict with one another.

Often their advice comes from a personal anecdote without fully considering why it had worked, whether it'd work again, or what could've been done better. They project from an experience and represent as prescriptive what was merely descriptive. Was success driven by those specific actions? Or was it due to timing, their position, or personal traits? Would it work for you in your situation?

This book examines networking from its most basic elements. Over years of observation and thousands of conversations, I've distilled it into five elements we can all apply in our lives. My intent is to frame these concepts in a meaningful and memorable way. To offer a common language shaping how we think and talk about relationships. To make networking more approachable for everyone.

The five elements of professional networking are: value, initiative, consistency, relatability, and credibility. Each element will be discussed in its own chapter. We will cover why it's important, what it entails, and how you can develop and incorporate it in your daily interactions.

To be clear, I am not prescribing a one-size-fits-all approach. Your traits, preferences, contexts, and needs vary from other people's. What's effective for you may not work for your neighbor and vice-versa.

While the five elements present a systematic framework, you are to make it your own. How you apply it should reflect your personal style. Be open to trying new things. Let's find what works for you.

First, what is networking?
At its core, networking is about developing relationships. It is going from strangers to acquaintances, colleagues, even friends. You meet people, learn about them, share about yourself, and grow closer. That's it. Everything else is a social norm or outward expression.

Yes, you do build relationships in your everyday life. Our focus here is on doing so more intentionally, regularly, and effectively to advance your life and career goals.

Let's clear up a few misunderstandings about networking. Some people feel that it's disingenuous. They envision smooth operators and politicians wheeling and dealing. Others think networking is too forced and awkward. The introverts among us would rather curl up with a book at home. And still others are content with their circumstances and don't feel the need to network.

All these viewpoints reflect a belief that networking is: 1) about self-interest and 2) an event or activity. Many people network for short-term gain. Unless they're seeking a job or selling a product, they don't think it's worth the effort. This view of networking couldn't be further from the truth.

Networking is not about attending events either. Most people envision this scenario: wearing formal attire, shaking hands, making small talk, and exchanging business cards. No wonder they don't like "networking." It sounds stuffy and uncomfortable. Like work outside of work. While gatherings can be great places to meet people, developing relationships is not confined to structured activities.

Furthermore, networking is not just something you do. Rather, building relationships is a part of who you are. With experience, it will feel less like doing and more like being.

So why should you network with others?

Many people say that it's to get a job. This is the most common response. Others point out that you should network *before* you need a job. They propose a more general answer: that networking opens doors for you. Meanwhile, career centers and professional societies promote the benefits of meeting like-minded people, keeping abreast of industry trends, and advancing to earn a higher income.

All these things are possible. In my early 20s, I would've been rattling them off too. Like many people, I used to think of networking primarily for career advancement. There are certainly seasons when your networking goals may lean toward uncovering opportunities and getting in with choice employers. But over the years, I've gained a much deeper appreciation for networking. Allow me to share three perspectives.

Networking helps you understand the world better.
Today I approach networking from a learning posture. It may indeed lead to career growth, but that isn't the primary goal. Through networking I come to better understand the world around me: how things work in an industry or profession; how people of a community think, speak, act, and live.

Knowing people is vastly different from knowing about them. I might've read about their line of work. I might've watched videos about their culture. But these are at best generalizations and imprecise outlines. It's one thing to be informed by a textbook or a documentary. But to speak with someone who has held a certain role, who has lived in a certain time and place—that brings the topic to life.

What each of us can learn on our own is limited. If we want to relate with people, there's no substitute for interaction. Startup founders must listen to customers to find product-market fit. Corporate leaders must walk the floors to see what goes on in their companies. Politicians and their staff must meet with constituents to understand their concerns. You and I would be wise to do the same.

Networking requires leaving our comfort zones—figuratively but often physically as well. We must step out of our homes, our offices, our social circles to learn and grow. As we meet people, we become exposed to new ideas and perspectives. We expand our worldviews and open up our apertures on life. We can verify what we had assumed to be true, and we are challenged to refine our beliefs.

If you don't branch out, your view of the world will be colored by a limited set of experiences. What you know and believe reflects, at least in part, the views of those around you: friends, neighbors, coworkers, members of your church or political party.

You become the company you keep. That's natural. But when all your information comes from a source or two, it can lead to insular, rigid thinking.

Our social circles can become echo chambers reinforcing faulty beliefs. Biases filter what we see, hear, and remember; they limit what we believe to be possible. It's easy to miss our blind spots. That's why we must interact with others. Exposure to their perspectives forces us to question our assumptions.

Moreover, meeting people helps us to build empathy. We start to see those from different backgrounds as individuals, not stereotypes and caricatures. We can acknowledge our commonalities and appreciate our differences. We come to understand a bit of their worlds.

As a man, I can't speak to what women go through. As an Asian American, I can't tell you about the daily lives of African Americans. Nor have I been gay or autistic or a refugee. What I know is what I've learned from friends in these groups. I will never say that I fully comprehend their lived experiences. But I've found that knowing a little, and openness to knowing more, engenders warmth and trust.

There have been times I held a certain belief until a friend helped me see things in a different light. Perhaps I was too naïve and idealistic. I was unaware of key facts and rationales. Or the issue wasn't real to me because it doesn't affect anyone I know—or so I thought. These friends challenged me to consider the issue with greater nuance and compassion. Dare I say, empathy makes us better people.

I'm not trying to sound preachy or oversentimental. Not at all. This affects our careers and businesses as much as it does our personal lives. If you have customers, coworkers, or employees, then you would do well to understand and relate with them. Knowing people from different walks of life offers a glimpse into worlds you may never encounter. As our workplaces and communities grow increasingly diverse, interacting effectively across contexts becomes imperative.

So networking can and does lead to career success—but not necessarily in the way most people think. Another important concept for your career is the velocity of information you receive. Let's dive in.

Networking helps you gain information more quickly.
In many cases, knowing information early is a competitive advantage: A job seeker hearing of a not-yet-posted opening can apply before others do. A business owner identifying an unmet need can be the first mover in the market. An angel investor learning of a new startup can participate in an earlier funding round. Simply put, the sooner you have the information, the sooner you can act on it.

Now information alone doesn't guarantee success. The early bird doesn't always get the worm. But the early bird has the chance to try or the choice to pass—and that is valuable in itself. Those who are late miss their window of opportunity. Or they must scramble to make up for lost time. In this way, by gaining information, you gain access to opportunities. You gain options and leverage. When that happens consistently, you develop a powerful advantage. Your successes compound over time.

For this to work, we must flip the script on networking as an active endeavor—something you do when pursuing a goal—to include passive learning as well. When you focus on networking for an active goal, that's like querying specific information at a set point in time. The people you ask may answer your questions and share relevant details. That's certainly helpful and shouldn't be overlooked.

But it doesn't tell you what else you should've asked or where else you should've searched. It doesn't represent everything you may find of interest. Therefore, networking encompasses what I see as a passive component to learning. Think of it this way: Even if you're not looking for anything in particular, you should still keep your eyes open. A strong network enables you to be in the know.

Consider two job seekers. The first wants to find a new role, so he starts attending networking events and coffee chats. He learns of a couple openings and applies to them. The second does the same thing, but she has also built her network over the years. Colleagues often send her job postings that might be of interest. She sees positions that her LinkedIn connections share as well. The former is limited to the information he currently seeks. But the latter has been exposed to additional opportunities over a much longer period. She is more connected and better prepared in her job search.

This concept is not limited to full-time jobs. You can learn about events and programs, contract work and volunteer roles. You can meet new friends and colleagues, clients and mentors. When you are well-connected, information naturally flows your way. Sometimes it's formal or systematic, coming from a company memo or an email distribution list. Other times it's casual and organic, mentioned in a passing conversation or shared by a friend in the industry. "Guess what I heard?" they might text you.

In my experience, those informal conversations are the most valuable. They are not the stuff of press releases and marketing collateral. They are not carefully worded emails and corporate social media posts. They reflect what people really think and feel. This is priceless. You can't get it publicly. Off the record, people tend to be more open and honest. So the information is more nuanced and useful.

Plus, when you learn of an opportunity early, you have more time to ask colleagues for input. You can do reference checks on people and organizations. You can find out whether their claims are legitimate. You can separate the wheat from the chaff, the signal from the noise.

Of course, not everything will apply to you. Ultimately, you decide what to act on, to investigate further, or to share with your network. For me, gaining information early and passively has led to speaking gigs, consulting work, and advisory roles. The possibilities are limited only by your openness.

Building good relationships doesn't just help us advance in life. It enables us to appreciate and enjoy our current situations—at work, at home, and in our communities. Relationships enrich our lives.

Networking helps you experience the richness of life.
Many people think of networking as opening new doors. That's a part of it. But it can also deepen existing relationships and enhance your present circumstances. The answer isn't always found in greener pastures. It's often best to tend your surroundings and appreciate what you have.

Years ago, I worked for a CEO who often talked about three keys to happiness: purpose, gratitude, and relationships.[1] I've found that these themes resonate widely. When asked what's most important in life, few people would say money or material possessions. While those are necessary, and we work to attain them, answers like family, friends, health, and calling are far more common. These represent our relationships, the things we're grateful for, and that which gives life significance.

Networking touches all these areas. Of course, through networking we develop relationships. But in doing so, we also have more to be thankful for. We find greater fulfillment in the everyday, the mundanity of life or the drudgery of work. It invites us to be more present in all we do.

According to Gallup research, most employees are not engaged at work. They just show up and do the minimum. In fact, many are "actively disengaged," spreading negativity to coworkers. For every employee who is engaged, two others are not. This is even more pronounced in some workplaces.[2]

Now this isn't a book on employee engagement. So I want to approach the topic from a different, more personal angle: What affects our job satisfaction? Compensation certainly plays a role. Growth and learning are important too. But on a day-to-day basis, there's no greater driver than our relationships. Do we get along with our managers and coworkers? Do we enjoy working with them?

Many employees quit because of bad working relationships—in particular, with their bosses.[3] As I tell job seekers, your relationship with your manager will make or break the opportunity. If you cannot work well together, nothing will compensate for it. A tense relationship adds stress and prevents you from doing your best work. I've seen talented people leave coveted roles for this reason.

A lack of relationships can predict low job satisfaction as well. Many people go to work and come home day after day without any meaningful connections. The job provides a paycheck—that's it. For some, that's enough. For others, let's say having a friend at work would make the day go by faster. Some people even stay in a job despite having better options because they like their coworkers.

Relationships, or lack thereof, also affect job performance. The project manager who has made friends across the company knows exactly whom to call for what—and they are happy to help him. The one who hasn't done so must spend time tracking down tribal knowledge and begging strangers for favors. Likewise, the new executive with industry connections can assemble a strong team and move quickly. The one without that network must rely on staffing agencies and consulting firms. Knowing the right people means that you can get things done in a timely manner, more effectively, or perhaps at all.

With good working relationships, we become more engaged and invested, positive and productive. Dealing with others feels less transactional or competitive. Our work becomes less task-oriented and more about the people. We are there to serve our customers and support our colleagues. In this way, we may find, or perhaps rekindle, a greater sense of purpose in our work.

When things go smoothly at work, our personal lives improve as well. We carry less stress home to our families. We stay present at the dinner table. We don't feel depleted at the end of the day. Rather, we still have energy for the people and activities that matter most.

Building genuine relationships is the same in your personal and professional lives. Networking surrounds you with dependable colleagues and lifelong friends. It infuses purpose into your work and reasons for gratitude into your everyday. Invest in your relationships, and your life will feel much richer.

Ultimately, this book is for the reader who: 1) delights in building relationships with like-minded peers, as well as those from other walks of life; who 2) wants to keep abreast of new information and emerging opportunities; and who 3) wishes to infuse color and meaning into both work and everyday life.

If you can identify with that, let's embark on this journey together.

We will begin with Value, the first of the five elements. Value serves as the bedrock on which all the other elements stand. It is the root of human motivations and the reason for our relationships. It describes what we want, what we give, and what we get. In contemplating the concepts of value, we won't just learn how to relate with other people. We will come to better understand ourselves.

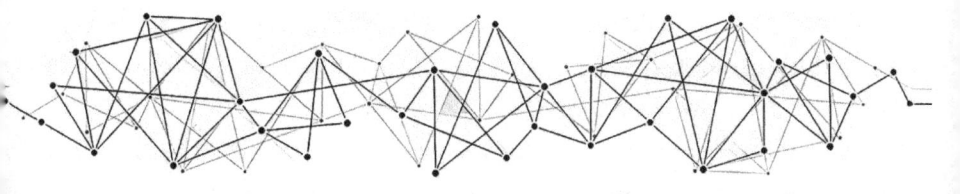

Element 1:

VALUE

Value is a strange word that means different things in different contexts.

When CEOs talk of "unlocking shareholder value," they usually mean increasing sales and earnings. This leads to higher stock prices and happier investors. In healthcare, we talk about moving "from volume to value," which means to stop wasting money on unnecessary care. Patients don't need *more* tests and surgeries (volume); they need the right ones (value). And in our daily lives, we might describe a purchase as being a "good value," meaning that the quality is high relative to its price.

Value may certainly be related to economics. Making and saving money are both strong motivators. But let's not focus on the financial connotations here. In fact, I'd caution against being too analytical. Not everything can or should be calculated. When we obsess over monetary value, we may cheapen or miss out on other forms of value. There are things we hold dear that cannot be reduced to a dollar sign. They are invaluable to us. We even call them priceless. Relationships are one of these things.

In our relationships, value is about meeting each other's needs. These needs may be general or specific, practical or emotional, temporary or ongoing. Different people fulfill different needs. Your boss, your best friend, your spouse, your pastor, your gym buddy—they each bring value to your life in different ways. You need and expect different things from them. In turn, you hold different commitments to each person. Some relationships are lifelong. Others last only for a season or a series of brief interactions. Whatever the case, relationships exist because through them needs are met.

Two types of value

There are two general types of value: The first is offering a solution to a problem. You may possess a crucial skill, a bit of information, a resource, or a technology that could resolve their issue. You can lend a helping hand or show them what to do. Perhaps you've faced the same problem yourself. With little effort, you can get them unstuck and on the right path.

Many people have helped me in my career. When I was interested in teaching, one colleague told me whom to contact at his school. When I started freelance consulting, another shared her template for contracts. Coworkers have taught me countless skills. Mentors have walked with me through multiple seasons. I am thankful for each of them. Though the support they gave me varied, all were undoubtedly valuable. In major and mundane things alike, they saved me time and set me up for success.

This isn't limited to our jobs and businesses, where saving time allows one to do profitable work. While that is good, people are even more thankful to save personal time. Productive work time is worth the earning potential. But personal time to spend in leisure or with one's family—that is invaluable.

My next-door neighbor once saw me outside whacking weeds and called out, "Chris, come over and get my lawnmower. That will take you forever." (I didn't have a lawnmower because I didn't have a lawn. But I did have a backyard full of weeds after a rainy season.) His simple act of kindness saved me hours, so I was very appreciative. You bet I would return the favor when he needs help.

The second type of value is being a good companion. This may be even more valuable than what you can do for them. Why do you talk with your friends? Why do you make plans to see each other? You probably don't need anything from them at a given time. Your initial interactions might've been as a solution to a problem. Perhaps you were classmates or coworkers on the same project.

However, you stayed in touch for a different reason. It's no longer to solve a problem. It's because you enjoy each other's company. Yes, value involves meeting needs. Sometimes the need is for social interaction and quality time together. In my experience, good friends are worth more than gold.

Dennis Kulp has been my best friend since college. He is one of the most genuine, hardworking, and considerate people I know. We had known each other since elementary school. But we didn't grow close until after high school. That's when you learn who your true friends are. Who chooses to stay in your life? Who makes the time to see you? Who shows up when you need help, when you're anxious and overwhelmed, or when your car breaks down in front of Walmart? After college, Dennis moved away to pursue medical school. So for a time, we didn't talk as often. Yet our bond remained strong.

Gina Lee is another close friend. We speak regularly and text almost daily. Gina and I can talk about anything. We feel comfortable sharing both the minute details of our days and the serious issues on our minds. There's a lightness to our conversations—no pretense, no fear of judgment, no pressure to impress. Contrast that with the fragility that characterizes many friendships today. People hesitate to share their thoughts. They're afraid of being labeled and judged. They feel like they must walk on eggshells around others. I'm thankful for friends like Gina with whom I can be my authentic self.

Ultimately, we enjoy being with people who are honest and caring; who are similar to us or whom we aspire to be like; and who are fun to be around. We are glad to know them, not because of anything they do but just because of who they are. We want to share moments and make memories—to do life together. In this way, networking is like making friends. That doesn't mean you'll become buddies with everyone you meet. But if you're a person whom others would be glad to know, you're likely to find yourself many great companions. It all begins with having the right mindset.

A mindset of value

What then is this mindset? It wouldn't be sufficient to say "be helpful to others" and leave it at that. Everybody helps *somebody*. That's necessary for functioning in society. But whom they help and why they help vary. Some people only help those who have helped them or who can return the favor. The recipient must have something valuable to offer, such as money, power, or connections.

Others aim to help anyone they can. Their help is rooted not in the recipient's identity but in their own. They help because they are helpful; they give because they are generous. Be like them. Keep watch for ways to do good. Cultivate a mindset of helping without expecting something in return.

Now some might ask: "How do I know it will be worth it?" You don't. Not from any single interaction and not immediately. But if you approach networking as a long-term investment, "worth it" becomes almost inevitable. Let me illustrate with a few observations on human nature.

First, nobody wants to be used. People don't want to feel like a means to an end, someone you hit up only when you need money or a favor. Relationships should not feel one-sided and transactional.

Healthy relationships are organic, characterized by give-and-take. You will help some people more; others will help you more. Those with a long-term perspective give freely and don't keep count. A certain person may never be able to return the favor. In fact, you may never see them again. But if you can, help them anyway. Help 10 people, 100 people, 1,000 people. Your rewards will come in time.

No, this isn't blind faith or karmic mysticism. It's because of a construct called reciprocity. Most people reciprocate, or mirror, the way you treat them. If you're friendly to them, they tend to respond in kind. If you've helped them, they're likely to help you back. You don't need to demand it. Reciprocity dwells in our sense of fairness. That said, the inverse is also true: If you've been unkind to them, don't expect to be welcomed. If you've ignored them, don't be surprised by their silence.

I learned about reciprocity from my great grandmother. She lived until 102 years old, so she had quite a bit of wisdom to impart. You don't live that long without treating people right. If someone shows you kindness, she said, then you should do the same for them. If they went out of their way to help you, then you better return the favor when they need it. To be clear, it's less about repaying a debt and more about respect for the person. Your show of gratitude is not a transaction. It's not an equal swap of value. Sometimes all you can give is a small gesture of your appreciation. Other times you pay it forward.

Now as you do this, you may start to notice a pattern. The people around you are caring and helpful, even the ones you barely know. You haven't done anything for them. So why are they helping you? That brings us to another truth: We tend to attract people similar to ourselves. As they say, birds of a feather flock together. Like attracts like. If you're an honest person, you surround yourself with honest people. If you hold a mindset of giving value, you gravitate toward friends who do as well.

Some people have huge networks, but everyone is in it for themselves. I'm sure you've seen the type: shameless self-promoters and slimy sycophants. On the surface, they seem to support each other. Yet their relationships are shallow and transactional, marked by attitudes like "I'll scratch your back if you scratch mine" and "You owe me one." There's no true loyalty. In good times, these people may land quick wins and appear to thrive. But don't be deceived. This is not sustainable. During bad times, when they are down on their luck with nothing left to give, they find themselves cast aside and ignored—just as they had done to others. Their fair-weather friends have moved on.

But those who help others from a mindset of value and a desire to do good—they will find kindness in times of need. Their friendships are deeper, anchored in shared principles. They are not tossed every which way by the winds of life. They stand firm through stormy seasons. This is the type of community you want.

So give without expectation. Help without hesitation. Start by listening well.

The importance of listening

The corollary to a mindset of value is a genuine interest in people. That is a theme throughout this book. Be curious about the world. Take interest in others and support them. Listen to understand their needs, desires, and preferences. Don't assume that you know. Let them tell you.

If you don't listen, your efforts will be blind guesses. Your good intentions may be misconstrued. If you send an article you wrote on a topic they don't care about, that's not helpful. It's self-promotion. If you critique their work without being asked, they may not appreciate the unsolicited advice. You intend to be helpful, and you may even be right. But like beauty, value is in the eye of the beholder.

Value is about relevance. When you listen, you learn what matters to people. When a friend tells you about a personal problem, she may want your advice, encouragement, or just to know that you care. To respond appropriately, you must first listen. Hear what is being said and what is left unspoken.

My friend Jordan Abel once commented: "Chris has a rare talent for forming deep connections quickly." This was high praise coming from someone I respect. Jordan is a federal investigator and a deacon at our church. He knows how to establish trust and rapport with people. So I appreciated the compliment.

However, forming those bonds is not a matter of talent but of practice. It's not an innate skill reserved for the few, an aptitude only of the fortunate. Anyone can learn to make deep connections. While quickness is subjective, when you honor people by showing genuine interest, you will accelerate any timeline.

Listening well makes people feel valued. When you listen, it's not about you and your agenda. Put aside your business cards and sales pitch. Give your full attention. Listen to understand, not just to respond or get to the next step. Don't interrupt or finish their sentences, and don't constantly redirect the spotlight onto yourself like: "That happened to me once. Let me tell you about it."[1] Sharing your own experiences is a natural part of conversation. But if you make it all about yourself, others will quickly tire of you. Instead, you want to speak in terms of their interests.[2] Ask questions and engage. Allow them the joy of sharing their stories and perspectives. Yes, make it a joy to talk with you.

If you read the last paragraph and thought these tips aren't novel, you're right. They are tried and true. Yet they are still uncommon in practice. So when you meet a good listener, it feels refreshing, doesn't it? Think of the best conversationalist you know. Chances are, they take the time to truly listen. Be this person to others. They will feel valued and, in turn, will reciprocate by listening to you.

When you take an interest in others, you grow more observant as well. You start to pay closer attention. You notice their needs and recall their preferences. This may not be a conscious effort. It happens naturally. What you do with the information depends on the relationship. But in general, people like to be remembered. A small favor or a brief mention—the little things make a big difference.

Pay special attention to the sayings they repeat, the stories they tell more than once. It's likely that these hold personal significance to them: an achievement they're proud of, an injustice they endured, or an inflection point in their lives. You can learn much about a person from the tales they revisit.

All that said, listening is not just about exchanging information. If that were the goal, there are more efficient channels. But you're not an order-taker, and life is not always about efficiency. Look at it this way: Having an idea of someone's intention is one thing. Hearing him or her say it is another. Even knowing what they would say is one thing. Giving them the space to express it is another.

In personal interactions and business dealings alike, the process of communicating is as crucial as the outcome. The emotional spikes act as relational glue. Trust and rapport are formed in the back-and-forth, the small talk and the deep discussions. Let us not be too efficient with our relationships, lest we miss out on building them at all.

Effective networking takes time and intention. It's organic but that doesn't mean it's impulsive. Just like an interview or a negotiation, it doesn't start when you show up in the same room. Opportunities favor those who are prepared to act on them. So how can you be ready? It comes down to having two things: self-awareness and helpful ideas. Let's take a closer look at each.

Knowing the value that you bring

You may not think you have much to offer. This is a common belief among both early careerists and senior professionals. So if you feel this way, you're not alone. And if you're like most people, you have more to give than you realize. Here's one problem: You may be too close to your area of expertise. You do the work every day. You know it inside out, so you assume that others do as well.

This has been called the curse of knowledge.[3] Imagine a professor explaining a highly technical process to college freshmen. In his mind, it makes perfect sense. He can visualize each step in vivid detail. But to the students, he may as well be speaking in a foreign language. They hear his words but lack the context and experience to digest the information. Likewise, what's obvious to you may not be apparent to others. You must recognize the value you bring from your unique set of experiences.

Let me pose a few questions for you to consider. You don't need to answer right away. Take time to reflect. Mull them over as you go about your week. Don't worry about having polished responses. This exercise is for you alone. As you reflect, don't limit it to your job description either. Try to distill what makes you stand out as an individual. These questions are a starting point to guide your thinking.

- Skills: What would you consider your superpower? What do other people say you're good at? What do companies hire you to do? What seems to come more easily for you than for others?
- Knowledge: What do people ask for your advice on? What kind of news or trends do you follow? What are your personal interests? Without preparation, what can you speak on for 30 minutes?
- Resources: What is your financial situation? What do you have that others need? Can you host gatherings at your home or office? What is your budget to join associations and attend events?
- Connections: What communities are you a part of? What activities are you involved in? Who are your mentors and advisors? If you were to start a business or project, who would support you?

Self-awareness also concerns character, which matters even more than knowledge or skills. How clear are you on your personal values? It's unwise to associate with morally ambiguous people because they are unpredictable. You cannot trust their promises. It's difficult to gauge their motivations. You never know when they have ulterior motives or conflicting interests. It casts doubt on everything else they say. Therefore, be a person of integrity and surround yourself with those of similar character.

Many people think of integrity merely as being honest—not lying, cheating, or stealing. It certainly is that, but it encompasses much more. Integrity is about a wholeness of self, an integrated identity, not one that is conditional or compartmentalized. This is the core of who you are. Your actions should match your words. Your behaviors should align with your beliefs. The things you value should stay consistent. It is who you are in the morning and in the evening. At work and at home. When no one is looking, and when everyone is watching. When you are in the majority, and when you stand alone.

The more self-aware you are, the more confident you will feel and appear. You understand who you are, what you need, and what you can offer. You're clear on your values and priorities. You know the type of people you want in your life. You don't compromise your principles trying to impress others. You neither demand attention nor beg for it. In short, you're secure in your identity.

Moreover, knowing yourself helps you relate with other people. Emotional intelligence starts with self-awareness. When you can recognize your own feelings, you will be more attuned to the needs and emotions of others. You can foresee how your words and actions will be received. You will respond in tactful and empathetic ways. As a result, you will appear more genuine, likable, and trustworthy.

Ideas for giving value

Earlier we described giving value in two general ways: 1) providing a solution to a problem and 2) being a good friend or companion. Now I will share a few specific approaches. For those who need ideas, I hope the proverbial light bulb turns on for you. This section is meant to illustrate the extent of how offering value might look. Most networking ideas fall within these categories.

Different activities will appeal to different people. Some will immediately click for you. Others will not feel enjoyable or worthwhile. That's fine. Your journey is not the same as your neighbor's. Explore and find what fits your style. Here are some ways to provide value and build your network.

Connect. In many cases, you may not be able to help directly, but you know someone who can. So make the connection. I've introduced job seekers and hiring managers; founders and investors; journalists and expert sources; event organizers and speakers; tenants and landlords. The list goes on.

On one occasion, a hospital contacted me to write ad copy for a marketing campaign. After reviewing the creative brief, I decided I wasn't interested in the project. At that point, I could've replied and declined the work. That would've been the end of it. Instead, I reached out to a colleague to gauge his interest. "I could really use the work," he told me, so I connected him with the hospital. He wrote to me afterward: "Thank you so much, Chris. I appreciate the referral more than you know." Even when we bow out, we can bring value to others. Through an introduction, both parties can have their needs met.

In other instances, the needs aren't as defined. You might connect two colleagues who share similar interests or two friends who would likely get along. Making introductions can deepen your relationships with both sides. After all, you're providing value to them through each other.

Now this is key: It should be mutually beneficial. Avoid making one-sided introductions, where there's a clear "giver" in the relationship. For example, you are friends with the CEO of a manufacturing business, and you meet a salesperson who asks for an introduction. He wants to pitch his enterprise software to the company. You might think twice before connecting them. You don't want this sales rep to bother your friend. Unless the CEO is looking for such a product, the value equation is not balanced here.

Be mindful of how you make introductions as well. Always double opt in. Even if it's mutually beneficial, check with your colleague first. Make sure it's agreeable to them before sending the email or setting up a meeting. You don't want to catch people by surprise. It puts them in an awkward position and may feel like an invasion of privacy. Guard your relationships as you'd want others to do for you.

Convene. Beyond one-on-one introductions, you can bring together people who have similar jobs, traits, or interests. Organize and lead the group. You don't have to be the preeminent expert. By playing this central role, you fill an unmet need for relationships. It creates value for that community and elevates your standing among them. This applies to both individuals and organizations. Startups and relative newcomers often rise to prominence by convening more established players.

Note the word "community" is thrown around a lot these days. People use it to mean attendees, subscribers, customers, and even prospects. It sounds nicer than calling them what they are. But it's not genuine. A true community involves shared activities that are purposeful, participatory, and repeatable.[4] Consider why these people come together, how they interact, and whether this is an ongoing need. As the convener, your role is not to be the center of attention. It's to facilitate those shared activities and relationships. Make it a worthwhile experience for all. That's the mark of a good community.

Curate. Whereas the previous approach is about gathering people, curation involves gathering information and resources. These may be job postings, industry news, how-to guides, product reviews, parenting tips, dinner recipes—whatever your audience is looking for. The common theme is that you are not the originator. You are not hiring for those jobs. You did not write those advice columns. The value already exists out there. But you add value by compiling them into one place, such as a job board or a newsletter. You make it easy for those who are interested.

That said, you don't just aggregate information. You make conscious decisions of what to include or not. To be effective, you must know your audience. Are they recent graduates or industry veterans? Do they want general news or in-depth analyses? Understand who they are and what they find valuable. Don't try to be all things to all people. Choose a niche and serve it well. Over time you may want to expand your scope to appeal to larger audiences. But be careful not to dilute the value you offer. What you curate must remain high-quality, relevant, and reliable, or people will look elsewhere.

Create. You may take a step further and develop your own content. This may be an extension of your curation efforts, such as providing commentary on industry news. Or it may be your original material and personal expression. The format you choose should be informed by how much time, money, and passion you have to devote to it.[5] Whether you run a blog, a podcast, or a YouTube channel, the goal here is the same: Create useful and engaging content for those who need it.

Use it as an opportunity to meet people. They may never respond to "Let's grab coffee." But they may feel honored to be a guest on your podcast or featured in your article. Now prominent individuals may not be interested until you have a large following.

They receive too many requests like this. Starting out, you probably can't book a world-famous scientist on your show. But there's a decent chance you can get another reputable expert—even an assistant professor from the same department.

People like to talk about themselves and their work. For some, it's an ego boost. For others, they are trying to build their professional reputation. This is often true for middle managers and junior faculty members. Your invitation is an opportunity to get their name out there. So they'd gladly say yes. The value proposition doesn't need to be for their employer—it may be for them as individuals. Understand their motivations. In this way, you can provide value to both your audience and your collaborators.

Celebrate. Remember that each person is the main character in his or her story. You're not the only one doing interesting things. So don't be too self-focused that you miss what's happening with others. Pause. Notice what's going on for those in your network; social media makes this easy. Compliment them on their recent article or podcast interview. Congratulate them on that new job, product launch, or funding round. These are all great reasons to touch base. Celebrate the good work and success of others. That affirmation may be what they need most.

Use your words to uplift them. A good compliment is genuine, thoughtful, and specific. It acknowledges something they are proud of—preferably a trait or achievement they worked for, rather than one they inherited. And ideally, it's a compliment they seldom receive.

This approach works for meeting new people as well. I once read an insightful article by an angel investor. I reached out and thanked him for writing. He responded: "Sometimes it feels like I'm putting the articles out into the void, so it's really nice to know people are reading them and finding them helpful."[6] As a writer,

I can relate. I've heard similar sentiments from artists and musicians, executives and educators. Can't access an academic research paper? Email the authors. Most would be happy to send it to you. Anyone who pours their time, energy, and heart into a project wants it to be appreciated.

Contribute. If you really like what they're doing, you can look for opportunities to get involved. This is straightforward for established causes and nonprofits. They may have existing volunteer groups, internships, committees, and programs for you to plug into. But even for informal teams or one-person operations, you can reach out and start a dialogue. Share your ideas and feedback. Let them know which aspects you find most valuable. See if they'd be receptive to your help.

Support them with your time or money. In different life seasons, you may have more of one to contribute. If you're young, you likely have little money but lots of time. Make the most of it. In college and grad school, I volunteered for a campus ministry, a community development center, a mental health nonprofit, a professional association, and so on. The lasting takeaways were always the relationships.

As you grow older, your time becomes increasingly scarce. You have more people who depend on you, who require your attention: your spouse and kids, aging parents and grandparents, employees and executives. Demands on your time add up. It becomes easier for you to give money to a charity than to participate yourself. That's fine as well. Your personal involvement will need to be more selective. But philanthropy enables influence over the causes you care about. It opens access to the people in charge.

The same principle applies to individuals and businesses. If you want access to someone, buy their product. Engage their services. Sign up for their workshop. It doesn't have to be a large purchase either. This simple gesture shows that you care about what they do. In turn, they will care about who you are. Likewise, if your friend is starting a business, open your wallet and support them. Many people will only give lip service or Like their social media posts. Your tangible contribution will mean infinitely more.

Whether or not you get involved, show gratitude when you benefit from the work of others. Express heartfelt appreciation. Most people are too restrained and reticent in praising others. You don't want to exaggerate, but there's no reason to be shy about it either. Send thank you emails, handwritten notes, and small gifts. If you've paid attention and know what someone likes, put that information to good use.

Guidelines on gifts

Giving gifts can be tricky. So I want to share a few guiding principles on gifts and relationships. First, gifts must be part of the relationship. They cannot replace it or make up for a weak bond. Giving a present *to*, or doing a favor *for*, someone doesn't equate to having a relationship *with* them.

I learned this lesson early in high school. I had a crush on this girl. Naturally, I paid attention to the things she liked. Her birthday was coming up, so I spent time searching for the perfect present for her. I thought about it for weeks. In hindsight, here's what I realized: During that time, I may have felt more invested and, in a sense, closer to her. But that was all in my head. There was no change in the friendship.

So it is with any of our relationships. A gift, and the intention behind it, doesn't substitute for actual time spent together. It doesn't compensate for a lack of reciprocal feelings. In fact, it may only highlight the one-sidedness of the situation. Nor will a gift, in most cases, transform a relationship. Deepening a bond requires doing life together. There's no shortcut for this.

Second, thoughtfulness matters. Gifts are given in the context of a relationship. So a gift should reflect and be appropriate for that relationship. For instance, what you give your best friend differs from what you give an acquaintance. What you give your wife differs from what you give a coworker.

By thoughtfulness, I'm not referring to how long or hard you thought about it. I'm talking about how specific that gift is to that relationship. Gifts can be thoughtful whether handmade or purchased, customized or off-the-shelf. The key is to notice people and make them feel seen.

One of my mentors wore a Disney necktie whenever I saw him. So I mailed him a Mickey Mouse-shaped tie clip, which he found a delightful surprise. Gifts don't need to be extravagant to be thoughtful. The primary value of a gift should come from its thoughtfulness, not its cost or economic value.

In contrast, the closer your gift is to money, the less thoughtful it is. That's because money could've been given by anyone to anyone. There's no sentimental value. It doesn't reflect the giver's personality. It doesn't require knowledge of the recipient. It says nothing about your relationship.

Plus, giving a cash gift is often considered poor form. It signals a lack of effort. It shows you didn't bother to find a real present. Imagine handing a coworker $20 in lieu of a birthday gift. That would be awkward. You should've spent the money on *something*. Even a gift card or a box of chocolates is preferred, because you went out of your way to buy it. That said, I'm not a fan of gift cards either. As cash equivalents, they're still fungible, countable stores of value—not the final present.

To be clear, there are occasions where giving money is acceptable. There are relationships where cash or gift cards are perfectly fine. However, they tend to be characterized by: 1) infrequent contact, like that uncle who drops by once a year; 2) a shared understanding, like siblings who agreed that cash is best; or 3) one-to-many distribution, like employee appreciation events. But those scenarios are not about building relationships. They involve existing relations where gifts make little difference.

Third, gifts should be freely given and freely received. The thorniest problems with gifts stem from misaligned expectations. If you expect a gift from your friend, and she doesn't give you one—or if its quality falls short of your expectations—you may feel disappointed and upset. You may question whether she cares about you. These reactions are natural. However, I'd caution against pinning such pressure on a gift. It's not worth harboring resentment, even if your expectations were justified.

Now if a terrible present is symptomatic of a one-sided friendship, you may want to reevaluate your relations. But the problem is not the gift. The problem is the relationship and emotions around it. So check your expectations. Hold them with open hands. Recognize that nobody owes you a *gift*.

Let's look at it from the other side. Feeling obligated to give a gift can also strain relationships. Suppose a distant coworker gives you a fancy Christmas present. Though that's kind of him, you don't think this relationship warrants gift-giving. You barely know the guy. So you don't want to spend the money on him. But now you feel indebted. You feel pressured to reciprocate, and it irks you.

What then should you do? First, realize that you are under no obligation to return the gesture. We must start there. Otherwise, any gift you may give loses its meaning. Second, reframe how you view the situation. You may not be close today. But perhaps this is an opportunity to get to know each other. Third, if you choose to give, then give with a cheerful spirit. That's the way all gifts should be given.

Bonus tip: Apology gifts should be perishable, such as flowers and chocolates. The rationale? You don't want the negative memory to linger. Hat tip to my old coworker Sara Tehrani for this insight.

How to ask for help
We've talked at length about giving value. Let's turn our attention to how you can receive value. After all, relationships go both ways. If you regularly help others, you should feel confident asking for help when you need it. You shouldn't always be the doer, the leader, the savior in a relationship. Opening yourself up to receiving help communicates that "I am like you. I don't have it all figured out. We need one another." Therefore, asking for help is integral to forming an authentic bond.

Moreover, when people have done a favor for you, they tend to like you more. They become invested in your success. They watch your progress and cheer you on. So how should you ask for help? Here are a few dos and don'ts.

Be clear on what you need. People can't help you if they don't know, and they won't spend much time to find out. They have their own lives to manage. So know what you want, and communicate it clearly. When you do that, they can quickly decide whether to help. For example, when you meet with a mentor or advisor, come prepared. Bring specific questions and topics you want to discuss. Guide the conversation. If you don't, your meeting will likely meander and not be as helpful to you.

That said, be open to other possibilities. Often people cannot grant your request, but they can assist in a different way. Hear them out. It may be the next best option. Perhaps they don't know the decision maker, but they can introduce you to her right-hand man. Or they might propose something you hadn't considered but would be valuable nonetheless. When you know what you need, you can decide whether to accept the help. Other times you should thank them for offering and politely decline.

Consider your relationship. When we were in college, my best friend Dennis worked at Disneyland. As a Disney cast member, he received an allotment of guest passes into the parks. Before long, word got out. Casual acquaintances from high school started coming out of the woodwork. They messaged him and acted like they missed him. But invariably, the jig was up within 20 minutes. They were just schmoozing him to let them into the happiest place on earth. Some even asked to bring their families or tried to buy the tickets for next to nothing. He was offended by their brazen self-interest.

In contrast, if I had wanted to spend a day at Disneyland, he would've made it happen. What's the difference? We had a relationship built through shared experiences. We had taken time to know one another. We had helped each other on countless occasions. The former classmates had not. They came as takers, not givers—opportunists, not friends. Their requests were disproportionate to their relationship with him. They tried to make a withdrawal without having made an investment.

Here's the point: Use discernment in whom you approach. Does what you're asking for make sense for that relationship? Consider the burden on their time and resources. You wouldn't ask a stranger to lend you $100. They would balk at your request. But a close friend may have no problem with that. Time is even more valuable. People have work, family obligations, and other commitments. They may be willing to help you up to a point.

Depending on your relationship, that may be 10 minutes or two hours, one-time or every month. There's no exact science, but try to exercise self-awareness.

Don't ask beyond what is reasonable for your relationship. People will feel like you're taking advantage of them. It comes across as ignorant and entitled. It hurts your relationship and reputation. Likewise, don't put them in an awkward position. Pay attention to their facial expressions and body language. If they seem uncomfortable with a request, there's a reason for that. For example, they may not feel like they know you well enough to refer you for a job. Respect that, and don't pressure them.

Make people feel valued. This is not a tactic—it's a mindset to adopt in all your interactions. Let it guide your decisions and permeate everything you do. That said, it holds special significance when you're asking for help. After all, people won't assist you if they don't like you. So be aware of how you come across. Treat others well. Never take them for granted. Whether it's a large favor or a small gesture, express direct and sincere appreciation for their support. We had discussed making people feel valued by listening well. Here are other ways to leave a good impression.

Show that you value their time. Be punctual. In fact, arrive early. Give yourself time to find parking and to get situated. Allow for unforeseen circumstances. It's far better to be a little early than a little late. Not only would others appreciate your punctuality, but you'd feel calmer and more prepared. This applies to phone calls too. If you say you're going to call at 9:00 a.m., then call at 9:00 a.m., not 9:02 a.m. Those two minutes may pass quickly for you. But they can feel like ages to someone expecting your call.

Just as you want to start on time, you should end on time as well. If you schedule a 30-minute meeting, make sure to stay within that limit. Start wrapping things up five minutes prior.

Now there may be conversations where it makes sense to go over. If that is the case, check whether it's acceptable with your colleague. Don't assume and ignore the allotted time. Being mindful of this shows others that you respect their time—and by extension, you respect them.

When you're asking for help, do what's comfortable for the other person. Meet them where they are, both figuratively and literally. If they ask you to email them, do it. If they give you their phone number, call it. If they have an existing process for scheduling, follow it. Don't try to be the exception or to assert your way. You want to remove all friction. Make it easy for them to accept your request.

Likewise, don't ask them to drive to your office. Go out of your way to meet at their preferred location. When you're there, make the interaction comfortable for them. Pay attention to the way they speak and act. Mirror their level of formality. Being overly formal puts unnecessary distance between you. Being overly casual can be off-putting to others. The sweet spot is to emulate what they do.

Don't make these mistakes. Avoid doing things that make people feel unappreciated. Of course, few do so on purpose. But lack of awareness can lead to regrettable faux pas. Here are several things to stop doing. These behaviors are ubiquitous yet distasteful to many people, so I find it necessary to include them here. While these aren't rules per se, consider them strong recommendations.

First, don't ask people for 20 minutes to "pick their brain." For some, these are disrespectful, triggering words—a demand on their time for no reason or compensation. If you have a specific question, they may be happy to meet. But if you want a general download, that's not a good use of their time. They had spent years developing their expertise. It's not there for you to pick.

Second, don't try to sell under the guise of networking. For example, don't immediately pitch after connecting on LinkedIn. They will view it as a bait-and-switch. Similarly, don't turn a "networking" call into a sales presentation. Be clear about your intentions. Sales is fine—hidden agendas are not.

Third, at the end of an informational interview, don't ask "is there anyone else" you should speak with. See, getting introductions is a great way to expand your network. But depending on how you ask, it can leave a bitter taste. They just spent time teaching and guiding you—was that not enough? Were they just one person in your list of many? Specify what you're looking for. Perhaps they had mentioned an adjacent role, and you want to learn more about it. Great! Ask them to connect you with someone in that line of work. Give them a specific reason to open up their network.

Now when someone does make an introduction for you, it's good practice to: 1) Follow up as soon as possible. You don't want to leave the other person hanging. It's your responsibility to make the first move. Introduce yourself and take it from there; and 2) Close the loop with the one who made the connection. People want to know that their actions had an effect. Thank them. Let them know how the conversation went. A brief note will suffice. Many people neglect to do this, but I believe it's only polite.

Fourth, don't pretend like it's an equal exchange of value. Put bluntly, don't act like you're doing them a favor. Yes, you want to talk in terms of their interests. And yes, they may derive some value by agreeing to help you. But just because they gain something doesn't mean you need to call attention to it. Avoid making it feel like a transaction. You would only highlight how one-sided the interaction is.

For example, I invited colleagues to be guest speakers in my class at UCLA. They all graciously accepted. They felt honored for the invitation and were happy to be involved. My students appreciated their diverse perspectives. I learned quite a bit myself. Now did the guest speakers gain anything? Sure, most told me that they enjoyed doing it. They were able to talk about their brands. Some posted on LinkedIn about the experience. But let's be real: They were the ones doing me a favor. It would've been tone-deaf to act like I was the one helping them. That's like asking a band to come play for exposure.

Finally, don't cheapen the interaction with money. Let me illustrate. A good friend is moving and asks you to help. It would only take a few hours. Yes, of course, you agree. You don't even hesitate. Now imagine that he or she offers you $20 for your trouble. What? My time is not for sale, you think to yourself. I'm helping you because I want to help you. I'm not doing it for the money. I'm your friend, not your hired hand.

See, your friend might've thought that giving you $20 is better than nothing. But that's not true. That's not how we operate. Involving any amount of money turns it into a transaction. So if you're not offered full compensation, then that's an unfair transaction. But the greater issue is that transactions are not as deep as friendships. Even if you were offered fair market rates, unless you're in the moving business, you may still balk at the suggestion. It's awkward and insulting to treat a friend like a vendor.

So you never want to do that to others. Take them out for a meal instead. Give them a gift as a token of your appreciation. Be thoughtful in your approach. Your friendship is more than your money.

When you are clear on what you need, when you consider your relationship and make people feel valued, they will be more than glad to support you. And when possible, return the favor. Remember those who have helped you. Strong bonds are formed in the give-and-take, the back-and-forth—the ongoing dialogue, the working out of your relationship, the exercise of reciprocity.

CLOSING THOUGHTS

I want to be clear about one thing: Not everyone will share your mindset of value. Many people only care about their personal gain. Their actions are calculating and transactional. Their friendships are fragile and fleeting. They value no one but themselves. As you seek to do good, don't let their egotism discourage you. Don't let their politicking distract you. Don't let their darkness dim your light.

Moreover, even if you do everything right, that doesn't mean someone will honor your request. Nobody owes you their time or assistance. Yes, certain people should help you based on your history together. But for myriad reasons, such as bad timing or misaligned expectations, they may not do so. Don't get angry or bitter. Harboring resentment isn't productive. Move onto the next person.

As an aside, one benefit of a larger network is that you don't over-rely on anyone. This relieves the pressure on others. And it soothes any hard feelings should they, for whatever reason, say no.

Ultimately, there's no formula. Each person is different, social norms vary, and times change. Here's what you can hold onto: Cultivate a mindset of giving value, develop a genuine interest in others, and make them feel valued. Do these things, and you will be welcomed wherever you go.

We'll now move onto Initiative, examining approaches for starting relationships. Opportunities don't just show up on our doorsteps. To improve our lives and careers, we must be people of action.

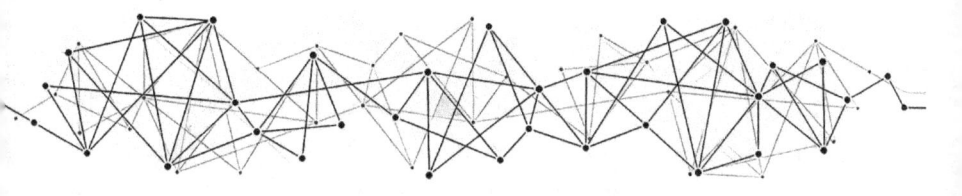

Element 2:
INITIATIVE

Have you ever tried a new activity and thought: "Why haven't I done this sooner?"

I know I have. Some friends in college invited me to go swing dancing. "Dancing isn't my thing," I told them, "I'm no good at it." One friend replied: "You just haven't had enough practice." She was right. Years later I tried it and wished I had picked it up earlier.

Your experience with networking may mirror this. It's fine for others, but it's not your thing. I've been there. I've stood at a proverbial distance. When I finally engaged, I was pleasantly surprised. Why haven't I talked with that person before? Why haven't I gotten involved with this group sooner?

This chapter is about taking action. A genuine interest in others forms the foundation. A desire to help them serves as a starting point. But good intentions aren't enough; they must be demonstrated. We must go and do. Relationships are rooted in tangible value, visible support, and concrete action.

Taking initiative expands your options. It positions you for serendipitous encounters. It increases your odds of success. As they say, luck is when preparation meets opportunity. By being proactive, you enlarge your luck surface area. You don't rely on life happening to you. You exercise your influence on it.

Of course, we all react to circumstances. When a need arises, we address it. When an invitation shows up, we respond. Most people in most situations are reactive. This is both natural and necessary, but it's limiting. Waiting for things to happen is not a reliable strategy—or a strategy at all.

Initiative is going above and beyond the average. It requires time, effort, and intention. That's why it's rare. People may not approach you at an event. They may not reach out on LinkedIn. If you do, they can choose how to respond. If you don't, a relationship may never form. So go ahead and initiate. The next time you meet, it'd be as an acquaintance or even a friend. Otherwise, you'd still be strangers.

When you take initiative, you present an opportunity for others. You create value both for them and for yourself. You might even ask: "Why haven't I done this sooner?"

Starting from square one

When you try something new, the first step can be the hardest. Why? Because it requires a change—a shift in direction, a break in routine, adoption of new activities. This change can happen gradually or suddenly. It can resemble learning how to walk, or it can look like breaking into a sprint. Whatever the case, you move from a stationary position to one of motion.

Getting started with networking can feel arduous. Many people say they don't know what to do. But often the problem isn't lack of knowledge; it's lack of confidence. When people feel equipped and assured, they spring into action. But when they feel unprepared or inadequate, they dither and delay.

Having coached many individuals, I've noticed two underlying issues: The first is unfamiliarity. Some people are very accomplished in their careers. They are experts in their clinical or technical domains. They make business decisions that have far-reaching impact. Yet when it comes to networking, they freeze up. They haven't done it enough, so they feel self-conscious. The unknown provokes anxiety.

The second, deeper issue involves self-limiting assumptions. These are the preconceived notions that hold us back. They are derived from or reinforced by things we've accepted at face value. For example, you may assume that you won't fit in with a group. You may think that you need certain credentials to be respected. You may postpone getting involved until you print business cards, perfect your elevator pitch, or complete other superficial tasks. These are nothing but excuses for inaction.

Unfamiliarity will pass with experience, but self-limiting assumptions are harder to shake. We all have doubts from time to time. We may have internalized unhelpful narratives that take years to unlearn. This process is not automatic. Overcoming our assumptions requires focus and discipline.

The first step is to recognize your self-limiting beliefs. See, they hold power precisely because they are assumptions—that is, they operate beneath the surface of conscious thought. When you pause to consider them, you will spot holes in your reasoning. You will see the inconsistencies and notice the disconnects. Once you've identified the core issues, you can start to work through them.

Here's a simple exercise: Get a piece of paper. Think of a goal that you've been putting off and write it across the top. Beneath it, draw a line straight down the middle. Now reflect on your goal. What is keeping you from moving forward? In the left column, jot down anything that comes to mind. Don't worry about having the exact words or complete thoughts. Unfiltered emotions can be useful here.

Take some time to review your list. Read and reread it slowly. Consider each line item and ask yourself: What is my main concern here? How do I know that this is true? Chances are, you'll realize that some of your assumptions may be inaccurate. Some of your self-criticisms may be unfair.

For instance, you may think that people won't take you seriously because you're young. I've been there. I once ran for public office—a board of director seat at the local health district. Most candidates were in their 50s and 60s. I had just turned 28, so I felt that voters might think I was too inexperienced. One of my mentors, Victor Carrasco, challenged this point: "Did anyone actually tell you that?" He was right. My assumption had kept me from boldly pursuing my goal. His question broke through my mental barrier.

Likewise, you want to center yourself on the truth. For each obstacle you listed, consider evidence to the contrary. Record these examples in the right column. You might think that networking events are intimidating. Sure, but you've overcome other challenges. Write them down. You might say that you're not extroverted or charming. Perhaps not, but you likely have a few good friendships. Reflect on those and take notes. Go through your list and address each of your concerns. The point isn't to reject your assumptions as completely false. It's to recognize that they are not entirely or necessarily true. Would having a certain trait be beneficial? Indeed. Do you *need* it? In most cases, the answer is no.

Taking the initiative to learn

Much of networking and career success comes down to this: Know a lot of things, know a lot of people, and make the right connections. Value is created in recognizing patterns and opportunities that others have yet to see—or at least have yet to act on. You might apply a solution from one industry to another. You might tell a colleague about an idea that they'd find useful. Or you might connect people who should collaborate. It takes initiative to put two and two together. Start with the initiative to learn.

There are two categories of learning. The first involves foundational knowledge. Read the seminal works in your field. Review the body of knowledge of your profession. Learn the fundamental theories, historical shifts, and emerging vocabulary. Don't assume you were taught everything in school.

When I was in grad school, I attended a lot of meetings. Often I would hear an unfamiliar term or acronym. I didn't know what it meant, so much of the conversation went over my head. Afterward, I would look it up. I would see how it related to what I already knew. Three weeks later, I'd hear the same term at another event. That time it clicked. I had an epiphany: If only I had known that term earlier, I could've gained more from and contributed more to the initial discussion. Looking forward, I could create and derive more value just by learning things sooner. That's why taking the initiative to learn matters.

The second category concerns actionable skills. Spend time learning how to do something new. It may be a financial analysis, a technical process, or a creative act. It may be adjacent to your work or an activity you're just interested in. It may benefit your current job or your long-term career prospects.

Then go apply those lessons. The real learning begins when theory meets practice, when the rubber meets the road. You may not feel prepared, and that's completely normal. You just need to get out there. Being tested is a crucial part of learning. Your results will testify to your strengths and your weaknesses. Take that feedback to heart. Nothing can replace learning from experience.

Learning isn't limited to long hours of study and practice. Knowledge can be consumed in smaller bites. In my graduate program, one professor drilled into us the value of environmental scanning—that is, keeping an eye out for what's happening in your profession, industry, and the world at large.[1] As we had discussed, the sooner you know about something, the sooner you can act on it.

I have a colleague who spends Saturday mornings looking through job postings at hospitals and clinics in San Diego. Are you job hunting? I asked him. No, he replied. He does this to keep abreast of the local market. He knows, for example, when a community health center is hiring for a key executive. That may hold implications for him or his organization. In addition, he skims the local paper for healthcare news from the past week. Your own scanning practices can be as systematic or informal as you'd like.

To stay up to date, I'm subscribed to numerous email lists. Some are daily digests from news outlets. Others are monthly newsletters from university programs, trade associations, community nonprofits, and so on. Most of these emails I skim and delete. But sometimes they include articles, events, and opportunities that pique my interest. I'm glad to receive those in my inbox. Now you might ask, what about following them on social media? Yes, that's the same idea, though it may require more time and scrolling on your part. That said, the channel isn't as important as the quality of content.

Be mindful of the information you consume. Not all content deserves your time and attention. Most email lists are not worth signing up for. Most organizations are not worth following. Demand quality. Distinguish it from what is merely popular. You want to get reliable insights and accurate data. You want to make informed choices and thoughtful connections. With quality inputs, you can produce quality outputs. But if your sources are mediocre or questionable, your results will follow likewise.

Let me be clear: Environmental scanning isn't just about news and events. There are always people involved. You don't just read about an innovative project; you can learn about its founders and leaders. You don't just hear about an upcoming conference; you can see who will be speaking there. Reach out to introduce yourself and learn more about them. You may be surprised at who responds.

Reaching out to strangers

Cold outreach is either welcomed or hated by recipients. Do it well, and people will respond. They will be glad to meet you. They will thank you for taking the initiative. But do it poorly, and they will hang up or ignore your email. For egregious offenses, some may even make an example of you on social media. So how can you be received warmly? First, you must see it from their perspective.

One of my favorite sitcom sketches comes from an episode of *Seinfeld*. A telemarketer calls and interrupts the scene. Jerry says he's busy and asks for the caller's home phone number to talk later. The man balks at the suggestion. "Oh, I guess you don't want people calling you at home," Jerry observes. No, came the reply. "Well, now you know how I feel!" *click*[2]

Most of us dislike telemarketing calls. Not just the "scam likely" ones. Even calls from legitimate businesses are a nuisance because they interrupt us and waste our time. Their messages are generic. Their offers are not relevant to our needs. Telemarketers have no interest in a relationship; they just want to make a sale. To them, it's all a numbers game. Pitch to enough people and a few will bite.

Telemarketers exemplify everything you shouldn't do in your outreach. You may nod and agree. But if you send the same email or LinkedIn message to everyone, is it any different? Take an honest look at your communications. View them through the recipient's eyes. Does this message sound like it was directed to you specifically, or does it scream copy-and-paste? Even worse, does it sound like it was written by an AI bot? If you received this message, would you take the time to reply?

People are more likely to respond to personalized communications. So tailor your message for each person. In your introduction, let them know that you know something about them. It should go deeper than the superficial "I see that you're a vice president at XYZ Company." Anyone can recite to them their title and employer. You want to show that you're reaching out to them for a particular reason. That you're not broadcasting a generic message. That you've put some effort into knowing who they are.

You might've heard of them through your environmental scanning. For example, you read about them in an article or a social media post. Reach out and mention it. Congratulate them on their success, or seek to learn more about their work. Engage in an honest and meaningful way. I'll give you two examples.

When I lived in San Diego, I heard of a local nonprofit called City Heights Coffee House. Yes, it was an actual coffee shop. But it was also a workforce development program founded by a guy named David Tran. A mutual friend had posted on Facebook about it. The concept piqued my interest, so I emailed David to learn more. We met up for coffee there, and he told me about their community programs and partnerships. He even invited me to a gathering at his house later that day.

On another occasion, I read a press release about YouTube Health. The video-sharing platform was partnering with hospital systems to produce authoritative medical content. At the time I was working for UCLA Health. I contacted YouTube's chief physician to explore getting involved. His staff shared about their vision and proposed ways to work together. They offered us a six-figure partnership grant. So I championed the idea within UCLA and introduced my colleagues to the YouTube team.

In these examples, my reason for contacting them was timely. I had become aware of their work and wanted to hear more. In other cases, you may need to find a topic to bring up. Look through their biography or LinkedIn profile. Read their posts, listen to their podcasts, watch their videos. Speak to something that caught your attention. The more relevant it is to your reason for contact, the better.

That said, tailoring your introduction isn't enough. You must go further. I've heard it best explained this way: Most attempts at personalization tell people something they already know about themselves. That shows you've done your research, but it may not compel them to respond.[3] Those in prominent roles receive dozens of messages like yours each week. They can't reply to everybody. Make them feel that engaging with *you* would be a good use of their time. Here are some tips to stand out.

Be informed and specific. If you have a question, Google it first. Asking basic or general questions reveals a lack of initiative. On the other hand, don't just regurgitate what you read either. The goal is to have your message understood and acted upon—not to flaunt your knowledge. Demonstrate that you've done your homework, but get to the point: What do you ask of them? Why now? As we had discussed, people can't help you if they don't know what you want. So make your requests clear.

Show appropriate respect. You can make one of two mistakes here. The first is to sound too submissive: "I'm so sorry to bother you…" Young professionals tend to write like this. Please stop. Many people find it irritating. Also avoid overused phrases like "hope this email finds you well." They sound soulless and disingenuous. The second issue is to appear entitled. Don't mark your emails "high importance" or otherwise demand attention. What's important to you may be none of their concern. Again, look at it from the recipient's perspective. Success depends on how you frame the conversation.

Then quickly deliver value. Apply the approaches we studied in the last chapter. A couple years ago, I read about Amazon's AWS Healthcare Accelerator. I reached out and met Amanda Goltz who ran the program. We discussed a few ways I might help. Amanda invited me to come speak to the upcoming cohort. She also shared the list of startups and offered to make introductions. I was intrigued by one called Grapefruit Health, so she connected me with Eric Alvarez, the founder and CEO.

That same day, I met Phil Brady, general partner at GoAhead Ventures. In speaking with Eric, I learned that he was raising a pre-seed round. So I introduced him to Phil. Long story short, GoAhead Ventures invested in Grapefruit Health. Now this was a win-win-win situation. Eric received capital to expand his business. Phil and team found a good investment opportunity. And Amanda could show the impact that Amazon's accelerator had on companies. It secured my relationship with all three parties.

Beyond direct outreach, how do you make new connections? Put yourself in proximity to the people you want to meet. Go where they are. We'll discuss events and conferences next. Here I should acknowledge that proximity comes more naturally for some than others. Those from affluent families tend to know people with wealth and influence. Those from working-class communities lack such contacts. For the latter, it requires more effort. I know this from personal experience, so I do not take it lightly. That said, I find that public events help to level the playing field a bit. They offer opportunities to rub shoulders with people you may never otherwise meet. Take the initiative to enter these spaces. Let me show you how.

Attending events and conferences

Many people are nervous about attending professional events. They're afraid of looking foolish or saying the wrong things. It feels like a performance, and they get stage fright. If this is you, recall what we discussed: First, question your assumptions. You might think that everybody else has it all together; everyone else knows what they're doing. Pause to consider: Is this really true? Probably not.

Second, approach the event as an opportunity to learn, not to impress others. Yes, you should put your best foot forward, but relax a bit. If you view it as a performance, you'll become preoccupied with your own thoughts. You'll seem anxious and distracted. Your self-consciousness will get in the way. But if you focus on learning from those you meet, you'll feel more purposeful and appear more natural.

Third, embrace the discomfort. It's normal to feel less at ease in unfamiliar settings. You're not alone. Even though I've been to hundreds of events, when I attend one in a new industry or different culture, I still feel out of place. Growth can feel awkward. But the sooner you dive into it, the sooner you'll get over the discomfort. As with most things, the second or third time will be easier. Your knowledge and skills may not have increased much by then, but your confidence surely will.

Now that doesn't mean you should come unprepared. You'll certainly learn from trial and error. But we can all benefit by learning from others as well. So let me share some tips. To be clear, these are neither rules nor a checklist. They are lessons gleaned from my own experiences.

For illustrative purposes, let's say you're attending a local conference. It's a daylong event with various speakers and panel discussions. These tips can be applied to shorter or longer events as well. Depending on your comfort level with professional events, you may read this section searching for new ideas to try. Or you may skim it now and reference it later. Do what makes sense for you.

Before the event:
- If there are people you want to meet, reach out to them ahead of time. I often connect with the speakers on LinkedIn prior to the event. You may want to contact the organizers as well. When you meet them face-to-face, they'll have an idea of who you are: "Oh yeah, we had exchanged emails." Some events also share their registration lists. I take note of whom to meet at the event, but I wouldn't contact them beforehand, unless there's a compelling reason to do so.
- If you have business cards, remember to bring them. Aren't these a bit old school? Perhaps, but they're also a quick, accepted way of exchanging contact information. Some people you want to continue the dialogue with will

- ask for your card. When they do, you should have it ready. That said, norms vary by industry. Some are rapidly moving away from physical business cards.
- Should you prepare an elevator pitch? I get this question often. Elevator pitches are helpful for organizing your thoughts, but you shouldn't be too scripted. Not everybody cares to hear your spiel, and you don't need to tell it to everyone either. Two people reciting their pitches make for a dull conversation. Share who you are and what you do. Keep it simple, and go from there.
- You may want to invite a colleague or two, especially if you're a member of the group hosting the event. This is a great way to catch up, while getting them involved in something you find valuable. If you bring people though, make sure not to abandon them at the event. You don't want them in a corner by themselves. But you also don't want to cling to each other the whole time. Find a healthy balance. Introduce them to your colleagues. Then go meet new people.

Start of the event:
- If you can, arrive early. It's not that you have to be on time to a conference. But running late can make you feel rushed and anxious. Those are distractions. Showing up early gives you time to get settled in. Find the venue, grab some coffee, use the restroom, and check yourself in the mirror. I also take a few moments to mentally prepare—to center myself after a long drive or to psych myself up for the day ahead. The best time is before the excitement of the day begins.

- Arriving before others is especially helpful if you're shy. It's easier to meet people as they trickle in than once they've gathered in groups. Psychologist Amy Cuddy advises getting comfortable in the space. As people show up, it will feel like welcoming them into your home, rather than being a guest in theirs. That's because you know the lay of the land, the schedule and the facilities, and you can show them. In addition, people are more eager to socialize at the start of a conference. Their social energy—and desire to meet people—wanes throughout the day.
- It's a networking event, not a movie. You didn't come early to find a good seat and wait for the program to start. This is prime networking time. Go meet people. To be clear, if you have limited mobility, please do what you need. I'm talking to those who get seated because they're nervous and sitting down feels psychologically safer. Remember you're there to network. If you need to warm up, go find a familiar face. Or talk with the organizers, the people at the registration table, even the vendors and sponsors. There's zero pressure. They are happy that you're there. Doing so puts you at ease as well. It's like knowing the host of the party and not just crashing it.
- When you're not approaching others, then look approachable. Don't stand in a corner hunched over your phone. Don't bury your nose in the conference booklet. If you look preoccupied, others won't approach you. Your body language invites them to come near, or it warns them to stay away. So be mindful of your posture and demeanor. Open yourself up. Be ready to shake hands and start conversations. Bonus tip: Hold drinks in your left hand, especially cold drinks.

- When it comes time to get seated, don't cluster with your classmates or coworkers. I often see a table full of students or people from the same company. I get it. Being with your friends is more comfortable. But you can hang out with them any time. At the conference, you're on a mission to expand your network. Branch out a little. Go sit with people you want to meet. Walk up and ask: "Can I join you here?" Or find an empty table and wait until others fill in around you. Here's a rule of thumb: Optimize for unfamiliarity. Meet new people. Get to know casual acquaintances better. If you had a choice between two groups, choose the one with whom you're less close.
- Make new friends early on. This gives you confidence and momentum for the rest of the day. How so? The two of you become familiar to each other. So later in the conference, you can approach them without feeling awkward, especially if they're with people you haven't met. Go say hi to your new friend and join the group. They will be glad to see you, and others may be eager to meet you. It keeps the conversation fresh when a new person enters the group.

During the event:
- When you meet people, what do you talk about? It depends. Did you intend to meet this person specifically? In most cases, it's a chance encounter. Neither of you knew of the other. Just say hi and introduce yourself. Here's the thing: It doesn't matter how the interaction starts. Comment on the speakers or the venue. If you're by the food or drinks, use that to spark a conversation. Then ask about them and listen. You may find commonality; you may not, and that's okay too.

- A popular YouTuber suggests this opening line: "Hi, I don't think I've met you yet. I'm [name]." This works well where there is some shared context, such as a professional society, a classroom, or a church group. It conveys two important things: First, people are expected to be meeting each other. Second, you are a social person who knows other people there.[4] This makes the encounter feel organic. It offers an accessible reason for why you're approaching them.
- If you're trying to meet a specific person, especially a prominent individual, strike while the iron is hot. Don't feel intimidated. Go introduce yourself and show that you know about their work. Ask a thoughtful question. Mention their recent article or media appearance. If they will be speaking at the event, tell them you look forward to their talk. It's usually easier to meet speakers before their presentation. If it's afterward, comment on something they had said.
- Make encounters count. Whether you spend two minutes or 20 minutes together, give them your full attention. Don't look at your phone or glance over their shoulder. Be present. Show genuine interest in the person before you. When in doubt, listen more than you speak. People may not recall what you discussed, but they will remember whether you made them feel valued.
- Help people feel included. If you see someone standing alone nearby, invite them to join your group. If they've approached your circle, take a moment to acknowledge them. You may want to have people exchange quick hellos. Or simply get them up to speed ("We're talking about…") and continue the conversation. But don't just ignore them or act like they aren't there.

- Bring the energy you want, and often it will be reciprocated. You are not the only nervous one. It's likely that other people are anxious too. They may act tense and overly formal, because they feel uncomfortable. They don't know how to behave, so they default to the uptight image of networking in their minds. But if you act natural yourself, it may help them loosen up.
- Know when to excuse yourself. That is, don't linger too long. Don't cling onto the first person you befriended. There's no hard time limit, but you don't want to stifle your companion. You're there to network, and so are they. Exchange business cards, if you'd like. Then move on. Say something like: "Well, it's been great getting to know you" or "I'll let you go meet others now." This applies when meeting prominent people too. Don't hog their time. Be mindful of others waiting to speak with them. If you want to continue the conversation, get their contact info.
- Some experts suggest setting a goal, such as meeting 10 people at the event. That's fine if it motivates you to actually do it. But be careful not to let that become your measure of success. You may rush and forge shallow connections. You may reach your quota and then stop. Or you may feel bad when you don't meet "enough" people. It's easy for a numerical goal to distract you from your true objective: to build purposeful relationships. Some days you'll meet many people; other days you'll meet few. Don't worry about the count. There will be more events.

End of the event:
- Some conferences close with a wine or dessert reception. Most attendees will have left by then. But if you can, stick

around. The day isn't over yet. I've had great conversations with people as we waited out traffic. I've met executives while walking to our cars. I've shared an Uber to the airport with a hospital CEO. Just because the official event is over doesn't mean the networking has to stop. Of course, you don't have to stay late every time. Do what fits your schedule.

- For multi-day events, try to grab dinner or drinks with colleagues. When people are in a relaxed setting—one not associated with work—they will show a more casual and personal side of themselves. That's when the bonding happens. Rather than seeing each other as titles and professions, you will relate as neighbors and friends. Your relationships will feel more genuine.

Events offer a unique opportunity to meet others organically. Some people may never respond to a cold email. They receive too many from job seekers and salespeople. But if they sit next to you in a breakout session, they may give you their direct line. There's something to be said for serendipity. When they have a personal encounter with you, they will view you as an individual—not just another request in the queue.

Launching a new idea
Events are great for meeting like-minded people. But what if the activity or community you want doesn't exist? Take the initiative to start something new. How? Let's look at the fundamentals.

First, do it yourself or with a small group. In many cases, you have what you need to begin. For example, if it's charity or advocacy work, nobody's stopping you. Just do it and talk about it. If you want to host an event, be okay with starting small. Not everything needs to make a splash. That's a fallacy in today's image-driven culture. Likewise, some people assume that they need funding or a brand or a formal location. The truth is you don't need any of those things. You can figure out alternatives.

Now it can take a lot of work, so find a couple friends who share your enthusiasm. Most people will sit out at first. They want to see things happen before jumping aboard. Some may even laugh at you. Don't get discouraged. Build traction, and they may come around, especially for the social currency of being involved. The first step is for you to execute on your vision. Lead by example. Do the work. Go it alone if you must.

Second, give people something to react to. Take time to organize your thoughts. Do the work needed to set things in motion. Show; don't just tell. Put something in front of your audience—the more tangible, the better. In this way, you keep the discussion focused: "Here's what I'm doing. Are you interested?" When you present a clear offer or request, you make it easy for others to decide whether to participate. They can say yes or no to concrete details, not a nebulous concept.

This applies in the workplace as well. If you have a good idea, do your homework, and then bring it up. Provide evidence and rationales for your recommendations. Be prepared for questions and objections. Whether you're calling for a new business strategy or a minor process change, make it frictionless for your audience. Make it feel like the clear and obvious solution.

Here's a tip from negotiation experts: Put it into writing. Concreteness adds legitimacy.[5] It shows that you've thought it through. It makes what you say more official, especially if coworkers have seen and accepted it. You may go a step further and come up with terminology or create a visual framework. Presentation affects whether your idea is discussed or dead on arrival.

In work as in life, most people take the path of least resistance. It requires more effort to counter your idea. So they'll go along with it, unless they have a threatened interest or other hang-ups. They may not share your passion enough to do the initial work, but they may support you in it.

Now that's not to say you should always take the lead. When someone else proposes a good idea, back them up. Second the proposal. Direct the spotlight onto them and make sure that they get the credit. Use the language they use to convey your support. Getting things done is more important than pride of authorship. In the process, you will make friends and build alliances.

Third, tell others what you're doing. This may sound obvious, but many people hesitate to share about their personal projects. My friend Aaron Byzak says: "Tell people what you're doing; they will either help you or get out of the way." In other words, you need to market your vision. You can't rely on the quality of your work alone to draw others in. The best ideas don't always surface. The most talented people don't always get discovered. You must take initiative to get the word out.

A few words of advice: Invite people individually to check out what you're doing. Don't send a mass message to 100 friends and expect them to respond. Some might, but most will ignore you. In this early stage, you want to send 100 separate messages. It takes more work, but it's much more effective.

Be honest about your intentions. If you're selling a product or asking for donations, be clear about it. Don't bait-and-switch anyone. It's better that they tell you no upfront, so you can move on. Don't pester or guilt trip them either. Some people don't want to join your group or follow your page or RSVP to your event. That's okay. Leave them alone. Focus instead on those who respond positively.

No matter what you're starting, look for opportunities to involve others. In part, you could use the extra help. But more importantly, it makes what you do more valuable. A one-person show isn't as engaging or sustainable. Even celebrities involve others in their work. Recording artists collaborate on songs. Talk show hosts find remarkable guests. Everyone is more interesting when relating with others.

Keep it fresh with new voices and material, while maintaining continuity with your style and presence. This can take various forms. Share the stage, highlight their work, or acknowledge their contributions. Whenever possible, let people tell their own stories. Enable and amplify them. The key to growing your platform is to involve others. It's also a wonderful way to meet people.

Organizing events is a natural way to involve multiple groups. Let's say you are planning a professional education program. Consider the benefit for attendees, speakers, vendors, and volunteers. Drive home the value to attract each group. Some people participate for a specific reason: to learn a topic, make new contacts, or market their business. Others get involved because they like what you're doing and want to see it happen. Coordinating events can open doors for many relationships.

Some time ago, I met a serial entrepreneur named Joshua Lee. He organizes events called Exit Hours, which began as weekly "office hours" for founders. It has since expanded to include investors and industry leaders. Now 50 people show up every Tuesday afternoon—there's even a waitlist! Josh's name came up in three separate conversations, so I had to check it out. It's an impressive group he's built. Because of his initiative, a thriving community can access mentorship and networking opportunities.

Perhaps you prefer smaller, more intimate gatherings. You can host a dinner for friends and colleagues who work in the same industry, share similar interests, or are just fascinating people. The value of the evening will depend on who's present. So ensuring quality is paramount. Andrew Yeung, called the Gatsby of Silicon Alley, recommends setting clear expectations on the purpose, timing, location, and guest behaviors. He sets firm boundaries as well: "If someone flakes on my dinner at the last minute without a reasonable excuse, I will never invite them to another event."[6]

Lastly, consider planning the event with someone else, so you can invite from different social circles and cross-pollinate your networks. When done well, dinners are an excellent way to deepen existing relationships. Fewer things build trust and friendship like breaking bread together.

Leveraging every opportunity

We've covered a lot of practical applications in this chapter: how to reach out to strangers in a way that gets responses; how to make the most of professional events and conferences; how to start something new and engage people in it. These are essential skills in your networking repertoire.

But not everything fits neatly into these categories. Networking is not limited to a few defined, standalone activities. It occurs in the course of your everyday life and work. Opportunities to meet people are all around you. In my experience, here are three key places to look.

Current activities. Consider your existing contexts. Think about your routines and commitments: the places you frequent, the positions you hold, the work you perform. With some initiative and creativity, you can find ways to build relationships through the things you're already doing.

I was invited to lecture about social media to nursing students. In preparing my talk, I contacted several healthcare leaders for their thoughts on social media use among clinicians. Most of them replied to me including: a health insurance CEO with a massive online following; a physician who had founded a popular medical blog; and a vice president of HR at a local hospital system.

I also posted on LinkedIn about my upcoming lecture. A few people replied and were willing to chat. One hospital marketer in Vermont messaged me because a mutual connection—a California government official I had met at a conference years ago—shared my post with her.

Now I didn't know any of them personally. So why did they respond? Why did they contact me? It's because I had made a simple, specific request that aligned with their interests. They wanted to share their views to educate and encourage students. So they were happy to speak with me. If I hadn't reached out, if I hadn't shared what I was doing, then the students would've missed out on those insightful perspectives. And I would've missed out on those valuable interactions.

Likewise, think about the activities you already do. Where can you involve other people? How can you help one another? What value can be created together? Take the initiative to make it happen.

New interests. Besides current activities, are there things you've been meaning to try? Taking up a new hobby or interest presents a great opportunity to meet people. These can range from marketable skills to leisure activities. That distinction is not important here. For instance, some people make a living with graphic design; others use it for their side businesses; still others do it just for fun.

Years ago, I became interested in media relations. It wasn't for a business reason, as I didn't have a product to promote. I just wanted to learn how it works, how people get quoted in the news.

At the time, there was a free service called Help a Reporter Out (HARO). Journalists, as well as bloggers and marketers, used it to find people for their articles. Some looked for experts who could offer advice and commentary; others needed laypeople to share their personal experiences. HARO sent out daily email digests of these queries. I decided to respond to the ones on career decisions. I wrote a career development blog and often spoke about meaningful work. So I used that as a testing ground.

My comments were first included in college blogs and job search websites. That didn't mean much, but it was something. I was getting my feet wet. Over time I contributed to stories in *HuffPost, Yahoo News,* and *U.S. News & World Report.* I was most proud of getting quoted twice in *Harvard Business Review.* But the true value wasn't in these media mentions.

The true value was in learning how to work with reporters—and leveraging that to engage other people. I asked friends for their input on relevant queries. I helped colleagues get quoted in the local paper. I connected journalists to credible expert sources. These opportunities existed because I had taken the initiative to act on my curiosity and learn about media relations.

What do you want to learn about? What do you see others doing that makes you want to join in? Certain activities are more interactive and social in nature. But you can meet people through any pursuit. There are always those who can teach and guide you; those who participate and learn alongside you; and those who haven't tried it but would gladly accept your invitation.

Competitions. I love contests and competitions. Not just because I like to win, but because I enjoy the energy and excitement they generate. Competitions draw people together from across schools, communities, and walks of life. Some are individual events; others are team-based. Some take place in person; others are virtual. Some, such as races and tournaments, involve activities you already practice. Others, like hackathons and ideation challenges, expose you to new things. Regardless of the format, they can be wonderful places to meet others with similar passions and interests.

Now this may sound counterintuitive, but competitions are not all about winning. Yes, you're there to compete and you hope to win. That's a given if you've devoted significant time and effort to honing your craft. If you're competing in the Olympics, for example, no one can fault you for keeping your eyes unblinkingly on the prize. But for most of us, in most contests, there is no such pressure. That singular focus is unnecessary, and in fact it prevents us from seeing the real opportunities.

Competitions are, by nature, short-term events. They represent a moment in time. Even if the process takes several months, that's only a blip in the course of our lives. Winning may feel nice, but its value is limited. Very few contests award life-changing amounts of money, record deals, and so on. In contrast, what can transform your life are the lessons and relationships you take away.

A while back, I helped to judge a healthcare consulting case competition. Though only a few teams won or placed, I commended all the students for participating. They gained that which is far more valuable: experience presenting to industry executives; feedback on their performance; knowledge and skills cultivated through the process; and confidence to face their next challenge, whatever it may be.

Moreover, the competition gave them a good opportunity to foster relationships: to bond with their teammates and advisors, to interact with contestants from other schools, to meet the judges and event organizers, to mingle with professionals in the industry, and to invite their friends and supporters. Unlike a typical networking event, which tends to be directionless, the competition had a clear purpose. This shared context provided a ready conversation topic and eased the way for interactions. Those who took the initiative went home with far more than a trophy, prize money, or bragging rights.

As they say, either you win or you learn. You only lose if don't take away anything from the experience. So I encourage you to look for and enter competitions of interest. Approach them not only with the intention to win but also to learn, network, and grow. For those tend to be the most lasting prizes.

Breaking from the crowd

As we wrap up this chapter, let's discuss the social dynamics. It's hard to take initiative, to put yourself out there, to go it alone. But sometimes it's even harder when you're surrounded by other people. How so?

Notice what happens in a crowd. People tend to emulate those around them. They look to the person in front of them, to their left and their right, for cues on how to behave. They follow in the steps of those before them. They conform to what the majority does.

There is an inertia to maintain the status quo, a gravitational pull toward precedence, a regression to the mean. Whatever the context, few people are willing to break the pattern. They don't want to look out of place, to draw attention and possible ridicule.

Change does happen, but it comes in waves. Imagine a party or a wedding reception where the dance floor starts off empty. As the music begins, most people are seated or huddled off to the sides. They glance around to see what others do. A few brave souls will take to the dance floor first, followed by their friends and then the larger majority. By the end, the whole crowd is on their feet.

Many people *want* to dance. But they don't want to be the only one. They feel self-conscious about standing out. So they wait until there's a critical mass before hitting the dance floor. Meanwhile, others didn't plan to dance. But it looks fun, so they decide to join in.

When you take initiative, you free people up to follow your lead. You indicate that a certain behavior is acceptable, even encouraged. You help them get over their inhibitions and act on their intentions. You show that it can be done—and that it's worth doing.

For instance, you may be the first to ask a question in a meeting. Or to walk up to strangers and say hello at a conference. Or to introduce yourself and drop your LinkedIn profile in a webinar chat. I've seen it play out time and again. Do any of these things, and others will follow suit.

Moreover, you can invite others onto the dance floor, so to speak. Your initiative extends an offer of friendship, community, or shared purpose. You give them an opportunity to enter new spaces and relationships. You let them experience a slice of your life.

Some people will need a little nudge. They won't just imitate you. They will sit on the sidelines and watch from a distance. When invited to dance, they will nervously respond: "This is my first time…" or "I'm not very good…" To be clear, they're not saying no! They *want* to be asked to dance. They want to participate. They want to get out there on the dance floor. But they need your reassurance that their unfamiliarity is not a disqualifier, that their fears and assumptions can be overcome.

See, initiative starts with you, but it's not about you alone. Your actions pave the path for others. So challenge the status quo and establish new precedence. Raise the standards and transform the culture. Inspire and invite others along with you. Initiative is leadership in action. I'll close with a final dance analogy.

Whenever I teach about leadership, I show a slide titled "managing yourself, managing others." It depicts an image of a dancing couple. In partnered dances, there's a leader and a follower. Now many spectators think that the leader uses his (or her) hands to make the follower turn and spin and move in certain ways.

But good leading doesn't start from your hand. You don't shove or drag or otherwise exert great force to move the follower. You move *yourself* and the follower responds in kind. The lead starts with your own body—your center of gravity, the direction of your shoulders, the frame you hold, the pulse you keep, and so on.

Likewise, that is what happens when you take initiative. When you lead by example, when your actions align with your intent—when you express it with clarity and confidence—followers will respond better to your lead, and the dance will be more enjoyable for everyone. Whatever you choose to do, do it wholeheartedly. Own your intentions, own your fears, and dive in.

CLOSING THOUGHTS

This chapter was about learning and doing. Those are two sides of the same coin. Yes, you learn and then apply those lessons. But the connection goes both ways. Learning is iterative and multifaceted. It involves action and feedback loops. In fact, you cannot fully learn without doing.

You may have heard of frameworks like plan-do-check-act or build-measure-learn. The stages go by different names, but the essence stays the same. You must test your hypothesis or implement your plan. Until you put it into practice, you won't understand all the challenges, nuances, or questions to ask. You can only learn these in the process.

Careful planning is indeed important. Yet plans may change. Circumstances do change. You may hold wrong assumptions about the path or the destination. You can have a perfect plan yet fail to execute. You can do everything right yet miss your window of opportunity.

A better approach is to be guided by the journey. This is certainly true for networking. Just start. Reach out to more people. Attend more events. Take one step at a time. Experience will show you what works and what doesn't. It will expand your options and inform your choices. It will bring you closer to your goals. When you take initiative and put yourself out there, it's incredible what can happen.

Next, we'll discuss Consistency, so your efforts aren't one-offs. Commit your lessons to memory. Confirm your actions into habits. The hardest part is getting started, so keep the momentum going.

Element 3:
CONSISTENCY

Networking is similar to exercise. Building your network, like building stamina or muscle mass, takes time and dedication. You can't expect immediate results. Nor will you see much progress if you do it once in a while, only when you feel like it. To see meaningful results, you must be consistent.

Consistency starts with commitment. Are you committed to growing and nurturing your network? We often say "build" but the more accurate term is "grow." Your network is alive. If you don't care for it, then it will weaken and wither. Just because someone is in your network today doesn't mean that they will always be. People drift. Relationships fade. Networking is a long-term investment.

This chapter is about developing habits and deepening relationships. Instead of haphazard and sporadic efforts, you want to create systems and routines. Why? Because by and large, we are creatures of habit. For most people, in most areas of life, it's easier to continue doing the same thing than to introduce change. This tendency can either make you complacent, or it can be leveraged for growth.

Let me illustrate. Suppose you're starting to work out. At first, you may hate going to the gym. You don't want to change your clothes, drive there, and perform strenuous exercises. You'd rather stay home, relax, and watch TV. Working out feels like an interruption to your schedule. You're not in the habit yet.

But as exercise becomes a part of your weekly routine, you find it easier to go. You even look forward to the gym. In fact, something feels wrong when you skip a day. If you're disciplined, you'd make up for the missed session. Going to the gym has become your default; not going is a break in that habit.

Yet if you continue to miss your workouts, then it becomes easier to skip more. You start to make excuses. Though you felt bad the first time, each subsequent lapse feels less consequential. "I already missed three days this month. What's another one?" Good habits die a gradual death.

While networking may not be as strict as your exercise regimen, the point stands. Be mindful of the patterns you set. When you make a commitment, follow through. It's not the plan or promise that matters—it's the execution. Let's discuss four areas in which you can be more consistent.

Showing up: Establishing a presence

In the previous chapter, we discussed attending professional events. Truth be told, many of us dabble. We check out a group once and, based on our first impression, decide not to return. Sometimes it's for good reason. Other times we nitpick at inconsequential things. Or we say we weren't feeling it, whatever that means. I've been guilty of this. In hindsight, I should've given some of them a second chance. Perhaps I had visited on an off day, and their gatherings are usually much better.

There's wisdom in going more than once. I've heard this advice given to people looking for a church: Pick one and commit to it for a month. Then decide. Why? Because on any given Sunday, the sermon may be forgettable. The music may sound uninspired. The people you meet may act cold. But stick around a bit, and you will get a better feel for the place. You may find that you like its style, leadership, and priorities. You may make friends and get involved in its ministries. Or after a few weeks, you may decide that it's not for you. Either way, you will make a clearer and more informed decision.

The same idea applies to professional societies. Give them more than one shot. When I began my career in health administration, I joined the American College of Healthcare Executives (ACHE). I've been involved with the local chapters for over a decade now. In that time, I've served on committees, spoken on panels and webinars, attended many events, and built even more relationships. None of this would've transpired had I left the first time thinking, "I didn't get much out of it, so I'm not coming back."

I won't sugarcoat it. Like most groups, the events can be hit-or-miss. The topics vary in relevance. Some speakers are fantastic, others are terrible, and most fall somewhere in between. Tom Dougherty was a mentor early in my career. He transformed the way I viewed and approached these gatherings. Tom once explained that he doesn't attend conferences to listen to the talks. He goes to meet people. For him, 20% of the value comes from the programming, while 80% comes from his networking.

Framed that way, it became worthwhile to attend even when I had little interest in a topic. If the event was nearby, I'd try to make it. I soon found an unexpected benefit of showing up: You start to build a presence. People begin to recognize you and view you as a part of their community. I've had many conversations start with: "We haven't formally been introduced" or "It's great to finally meet you." Those people felt less like strangers and more like friends of a friend.

Being consistent starts with how you view your role. Are you a visitor or a member, a spectator or a participant? Do you identify with this group? Do you want to see it grow and thrive? A casual attendee may be treated as a guest. But if you consider it your professional home, then roll up your sleeves. Look for opportunities to serve. Welcome those who are new or on the fringes. Contribute to your community. Build lasting relationships as you work toward a common purpose.

Meet the leaders and see how you can get involved. At the local level, professional associations are run by volunteers. So they always need help. Some groups are well-established. You can join their programs or membership committees. Many groups, however, are fairly inactive. They would like to do more for their members. If you notice a gap, take initiative and propose what you can offer. Randy Pausch advises in *The Last Lecture*: "Have something to bring to the table. That makes you more welcome."[1]

I demonstrated this when I joined the Venture Cooperative, a virtual learning community by Laconia Capital Group. My main goal was to build relationships with the Laconia investment team. Early on, I was anonymous, one of 200 online participants. Yet I knew I could stand out. I knew I had value to offer. They don't know me yet, I thought, but they will. I learned about their investment thesis and started sharing deal flow with them. Soon enough, managing partner Geri Kirilova remarked that I was the "most prolific fellow by an order of magnitude." Several months later, they invested in a startup I had sourced. When you have something to offer, and you show up consistently, people will take notice.

If you're involved in multiple communities, consider the intersections between them. Cross-pollinate your resources and relationships. Find ways to touch adjacent fields. For instance, I worked on the business side of healthcare for over a decade. I routinely dealt with finance and reimbursement issues. But when I presented to nursing or pharmacy groups, that information was novel to many. Those who found it valuable reached out to talk further. In the process, I learned from them as well.

At some point you may wish to step into a leadership role. Whether elected or appointed, being a leader can have an outsized effect on your networking. You'll have even more opportunities to meet and work with others. Consistency matters here as well. To be placed into a position of influence, you must first build trust. It's not just about your skills or credentials. Show that you're reliable and committed to the cause. That comes from your ongoing involvement with the group.

Several opportunities became available to me because I had established my presence. I had been around and brought value to those groups over time. So I was top of mind when a need arose. Here are three of my involvements at the time of writing.

First, I'm a participant ambassador for the NIH All of Us Research Program. This is a federal initiative to advance medical research by including historically underrepresented groups in clinical trials. For several years, I had volunteered at the local level through Scripps Research in San Diego. So when the national advisory team sought new members, the program leaders at Scripps nominated me.

Second, I'm a lecturer at the UCLA Fielding School of Public Health. When I worked for the UCLA medical center, I had spent time getting to know the campus side. I had spoken in classes and at student events. So when they needed someone to facilitate a healthcare marketing course, one professor suggested to the program director: "What about Chris Lee?" They reached out and asked me to teach.

Third, I'm a venture partner at GoAhead Ventures, the firm I mentioned in the previous chapter. I had continued scouting for startups and building relationships with the general partners (GPs). They had invested in a couple deals I sourced early on, which got me on their radar. A few months later, they launched the venture partner program and invited me into the first cohort.

This role has taught me another lesson about showing up. As a venture partner, I'm invited to sit in on all the startup pitches to our GPs. They share the schedule ahead of time each week. At first, I only attended the healthtech and SaaS pitches. But GP Clancey Stahr encouraged me to come to more—not just the ones where I had domain expertise. It gives you a "Renaissance man education," as he put it. That was an aha moment for me. Sometimes the value for you is there; you just need to show up.

Beyond formal roles and professional groups, volunteering is a great way to meet people who share your passions. Whether you want to end world hunger, care for cancer survivors, or support girls in STEM careers, you will find others working toward a similar vision. Join them. Bond as you make the world a better place. Another benefit is that it helps you build a diverse network. Through volunteer activities, I've met people from across different life stages, lines of work, and walks of life.

Now consistency is incomplete without intentionality. Not all communities are created equal. Not all groups are worth your time. Every decision has its opportunity costs. So be invested but not inflexible, steadfast but not stubborn. Recognize when you're on a dead-end path, when you're spread too thin, or when you've lost interest in a pursuit. Your commitment is not to a specific activity—it's to building relationships and growing your network. Prune away that which isn't conducive to your goals.

When you prune a plant, you trim away unwanted branches or stems. Usually, it's because they're dead, dying, or overgrown in the wrong places. Cutting away these parts isn't harmful to the plant. On the contrary, you support its growth in the right direction. You accelerate its fruitfulness.

Several years ago, I was active in many causes and communities. Some of them no longer served the purpose that they once had for me. That's not to say they were no longer good or worthy endeavors. Nor does it speak to the ability or devotion of the people involved. But there is a time for everything, and it was time to let them go. If I wanted to be effective, I needed to focus. I needed to make a conscious decision about where to invest my time and energy. I needed to be fully present.

Showing up regularly establishes a presence. The whole (making consistent efforts) becomes greater than the sum of its parts (attending one-off events). People notice when you're there. They notice what you say and do. They notice how you treat others. And if you've contributed to the group and made your presence known, they will also notice and feel your absence.

Following up: Staying top of mind
Beyond a general presence, you want people to remember you specifically—to keep you in mind for new opportunities and

things of interest. Just because you met at an event doesn't mean they will recognize you later. You were one of dozens of new faces. They may recall meeting you. But awareness that you exist is a far cry from a relationship. To be remembered, you must follow up.

The initial follow-up. After meeting someone you may want to know further, send an email or a LinkedIn connection request. Write a personal note. Remind them where they had met you. Mention something you had discussed. Not only does this jog their memory to respond, but when you look back on it, you'll remember how you know them. Otherwise, your "connection" is just a number.

With those you want to continue talking with, schedule a call or a meetup. Coffee or lunch are better than workplace meetings. When people leave the office, they're in a different mindset. They tend to be more relaxed and approachable, more at ease to speak their minds. You can get to know someone better over a meal than in months of meetings. They're more likely to remember the interaction as well.

If you had made any commitments—such as sending information or making an introduction—remember to follow through. Likewise, if they had agreed to something, help them keep their promise. Follow up and get the ball rolling. Even if there's no set timeline, email them to document what you had discussed. Suppose they had expressed interest in doing business together. They may have forgotten they said that. If you have a written exchange, you can point to it later. That's much better than starting over from square one. It's also useful in case their gatekeeper tries to deny you a meeting.

Now sometimes you won't get a response to your follow-up. This happens to all of us, regardless of how smart, skilled, or senior you are. Don't get discouraged, and don't make assumptions. A delay doesn't mean they're no longer interested. Nor does it signify that you said or did anything wrong. People are busy. Life happens. They may have missed your email or voicemail. Reach out again. Now use your best judgment on how many times to follow up. If you don't hear back after several attempts, you may want to bow out. Stop bothering them. But leave the door open in case they're still interested.

In some cases, people will follow up with you first. You want to acknowledge it and respond promptly. Responsiveness is an underrated trait, vital for doing business and building relationships.

First, being responsive captures opportunities. It recognizes the value and seizes the moment. In contrast, those who delay will miss their chance. Impatient customers will go elsewhere. Job candidates will accept other offers. Reporters will move onto the next story. People don't have time to wait around—they likely have other options.

Second, being responsive reassures people. It lets them know that their message has been received. It shows that you value their involvement. It keeps them in the loop. Communications don't need to be frequent; they just need to be timely. Slowness to respond introduces uncertainty. It puts a relationship into question. People want to know where they stand with you.

So be responsive. If you are going to do something anyway, there's no reason to procrastinate. Do it as soon as possible. Make that bit more effort. In my experience, the upside is well worth it.

Nurturing connections. Keeping in touch is an essential yet neglected part of relationships. Most of us have room to improve in this area. Building relationships takes time. I'm not referring to a specific period like six or 12 months. Time itself doesn't equate to closeness; we all have long-time colleagues we barely know. But without interactions over time, there would be no trust and rapport. Consistency turns points into lines, snapshots into stories, first impressions into familiarity into friendships.

What constitutes regular contact varies across relationships. You may talk with some people once a month, others once a quarter, and still others once a year. It's not about the frequency. More is not necessarily better. In fact, Stanford researchers have found that "people with whom you have [moderately weak] ties are more likely to have information or connections" that are helpful to your career mobility. Their networks are less likely to overlap with yours, which opens up new possibilities.[2]

Staying in touch will happen naturally with some people, but in many cases, you must create those touchpoints. Reach out when you start a new job, when you see them get promoted, or upon other trigger events. Use the opportunity to catch up. But don't limit your outreach to those big moments. Ping them to share something they might appreciate: an article, an event, or a quote. You can do this any time. It shows thoughtfulness on your part. I also like to send a quick message when someone wins an award, speaks at a conference, or gets quoted in the news. Find reasons to interact.

To form a relationship, emails and LinkedIn messages are fine to start. They may be your primary means of contact with a new colleague. But you don't want them to be your *only* modes of communication. Asynchronous written text is great for a paper trail and efficient for work, yet it's too slow and impersonal for most relationships. Take it offline. Engage more senses. People are more likely to remember those with whom they've interacted multiple times—but also in multiple ways.

If you've only corresponded by email, especially for work, they may not recognize you outside that context. It's also unlikely that you know much about one another. Contrast that with a phone call. In a few minutes, you can learn more about each other than over a dozen emails. You can sense tone and emphasis and hesitation. You can build rapport more easily in real time.

Make it a video call, and you can read visual cues as well: facial expressions, hand gestures, and body language. You can watch their reactions as you speak. Are they nodding and smiling? Or are they frowning and furrowing their brows? That immediate feedback tells you whether your message is landing well or if you need to adjust your approach. In addition, pauses feel less awkward. You can see what your companion is doing as you wait for their response. I've found that video calls are especially helpful for initial meetings or serious conversations.

Likewise, getting together in person can be extremely beneficial. That doesn't mean you always need to meet physically. Nor does it mean your in-person relationships are all stronger than those formed online. But breaking bread together, sharing an activity, or occupying the same room can make someone feel more real and memorable. You get a better sense of them by their posture, eye contact, and handshake. The subtlest details may inform your impression and help you answer: "Do I like and trust this person?"

Spending time together informally can be telling. At an important meeting, people are on their best behavior. They watch their every word and project a polished image. But outside structured situations, you start to see who they truly are. You observe how they treat other people—their families, waitstaff, and those who are different from them. You hear what they say off the record. To be clear, this isn't about finding fault. It's simply doing life together. If you surround yourself with good company, you'd likely gain respect for them. You'd share unplanned moments that become the stories revisited years later. Casual environments strengthen bonds, as colleagues become friends.

Ultimately, how you stay in touch depends on the relationship. There are numerous channels these days. I contact certain people through email, others by phone or text, and still others on LinkedIn, Messenger, or another platform. People have different communication preferences. And the formality of your relationships varies. Do what feels natural and appropriate for each one.

Maintaining ties. So far, we've talked about starting and nurturing new relationships. Now I want to call attention to preserving old connections—with former classmates, coworkers, and so on. These are characteristically different from active relationships. After leaving a job, for example, most people lose touch with their old boss and coworkers. It's natural to drift when you have fewer reasons to interact. But old colleagues may be some of your best supporters. They know you. They've seen your work. By touching base once every few months, you can keep those relationships alive.

At times you may need them to vouch for you. One hiring manager asked me to submit three letters of recommendation by the next day. Not listing my references, mind you, but turning in formal letters. I hate bothering people on short notice. In school, we had to ask professors weeks ahead. I expressed hesitation about the timeline. The hiring manager replied that if I was who I represented myself to be—with all my experience and involvements—I should have no problem getting those letters.

As we hung up, I got to work texting and emailing people. The tricky part was finding those who had worked with me in a relevant function *and* who might write me a letter in the next 24 hours. Thankfully, with a little determination and a lot of grace, I turned in three glowing letters by the next day. This episode reminded me why it's important to maintain relationships. Recommendations on short notice don't come from casual acquaintances. They come from those you may call friends.

When I say "friends" here, I don't just mean your former peers. Yes, being in a similar career or life stage fosters connection. It's natural to be friends with your classmates and coworkers. But another group to remember are those ahead of you: your teachers, mentors, and advisors. I've found that most are happy to stay in touch. You may have known them in those formal roles for a brief time. Afterward, however, the nature of these relationships may evolve—from one-way guidance to mutual learning and respect. From scheduled meetings to impromptu calls. From formality to friendship.

I'm grateful for my past teachers and mentors. From time to time, I share life updates with them or seek their advice. They continue to be a sounding board, providing wise counsel and encouragement. As I've progressed in my career, they have reached out to me for help as well. One mentor was working on a consulting project and asked me about pharmacy economics. Another was considering a job offer and wanted my thoughts on the organization. I've helped others land speaking gigs, recruit talent, and meet potential clients. Over time we've become more like colleagues and friends.

Reconciling relationships. Unfortunately, relationships aren't all sunshine and rainbows. At times we must share bad news, own up to our mistakes, confront others about their actions, or clarify a misunderstanding. These situations occur both at work and in our personal lives. They are unpleasant. But how we handle them affects our relationships and reputations. It shapes our habits and even how we view ourselves.

The first step is choosing to engage in these difficult conversations. It's easier to run. It's easier to ignore the problem or the person. In our digital age, it's especially convenient to "ghost" or block others. Most people would prefer to avoid conflict. But when dealt with in a mature, respectful manner, the result is often better emerging from a difficult, mutually intentional talk.

I'm not saying that it will always work out. Sometimes problems will remain unresolved, relationships unreconciled. Sometimes others will reject what we have to say. But even then, we tend to be glad to have had those conversations, to clear the air and find closure.

So learn to have difficult conversations. No ghosting, no gossiping, no beating around the bush. Let go of your pride. Apologize for your faults. Address issues directly and with tact—as one mature adult to another. They might not like what you have to say, but most people will appreciate the honesty and respect you for it. Likewise, you can walk away respecting yourself.

Reconciliation is more than conflict resolution. This distinction is key. When you pursue reconciliation, you focus on restoring the relationship and honoring the individual—not merely on solving the problem. In fact, the problem becomes secondary. You may need to work through specific issues together. But if both sides value and prioritize the relationship, all wrongs can be forgiven. All wounds will soon heal. It's often more prudent to mend a small rift than to let a relationship fall apart.

Reconnecting with others. Now what if you had lost touch? What if it has been years since you've spoken? You may feel a bit awkward to contact them. First, recognize that they may feel the same way. If neither takes the initiative, then that reunion would never happen. Second, people tend to be more receptive than you may assume. Even if you weren't close, they may be happy to see your name or hear a familiar voice. Don't overthink it. The worst that can happen is that they don't respond.

So let go of your hang-ups. You may remember that argument, but they may not. You may recall that embarrassing episode, but they probably don't. What's emotionally significant—and therefore, memorable—to you, may hold less weight to them. With the passing of time, most quarrels are forgotten. Most offenses are forgiven. Let bygones be bygones, as they say. In any case, people have fuzzy memories. Unless you were close, they may not remember much about you either good or bad.

Find reasons to reconnect. Here are three ideas that are especially suited for this: 1) Send them holiday wishes. Holidays are natural occasions to reach out and catch up; 2) Invite them to a gathering. Planning an event or reunion creates value for all involved; and 3) Share about the influence they've had on you. Now and then, I'm reminded of what someone had said or done. Their words stuck with me, or their actions left an impression. So I let them know. People like hearing about the impact they've made.

Now don't expect to restore a relationship to the way it was. Think of it as starting a new relationship with an old contact. For example, when you see a college roommate 10 years later, you may reminisce and try to rekindle a friendship. But it will undoubtedly be different. In some cases, you may grow closer than you used to be. In other cases, you may interact only on occasion. That's natural. You both have grown and changed over time. You now have different needs, interests, and responsibilities.

Lastly, if you have a request, don't beat around the bush. It makes people uneasy. They may be wary that you will pitch them a pyramid scheme, a life insurance policy, or a new religion. Unfortunately, that's often the case when old contacts message out of the blue. Many of us have been on the receiving end of those awkward encounters. So clear the air and put them at ease. Get to the point quickly.

Keeping up: Compounding your results

Every week I meet people who are starting a new activity. Some are writing articles or making videos. Others are organizing local or virtual events. Still others are posting on LinkedIn for the first time. As we had discussed, starting something new can be a great way to gain visibility and expand your network. But success doesn't happen overnight, and most people give up too early.

They launch a blog, podcast, or YouTube channel and excitedly tell everyone. In the first month, they post several times a week. Encouraged by their friends' support, or at least curiosity, they feverishly create content. They spend hours planning their next masterpiece. But as the initial interest wanes, so does their fervor. Their publishing schedule drops to once a week, once every couple weeks, then once a month. It soon fizzles out. Or it becomes so sporadic that they never gain traction.

People overestimate their willpower and underestimate the work it takes. Starting is the relatively easy part. It seems like everyone is doing something these days. But being consistent, sustaining the effort, and making real progress are much rarer. Few are prepared to put in the time and effort needed. When they don't see immediate results—in terms of Likes, followers, sales, or praise—they lose motivation.

On the one hand, that's understandable. When you organize an event and only five people register—and two of them don't even show up—it can be disheartening. When you spend hours writing, recording, and producing a video, and half the views on it are your own, you may wonder why you even bother. Your efforts go unappreciated. You feel unseen. You're on a lonely stage playing to an empty room.

On the other hand, it's a common, expected struggle. When you do anything worthwhile, you must keep at it. It takes time to hone your skills, develop your style, or spread the word. People may be uninterested or skeptical at first. Getting their attention and convincing them requires diligence, tenacity, and an unyielding belief that what you do matters. If you don't care enough to continue, why should they?

But if you're consistent, people will start to pay attention. They see when you post things, even if they didn't Like it. They notice your good work, even if they didn't say anything. And over time more people will know who you are, even if they haven't met you. Often you don't need to be the smartest or most creative person to stand out. You must simply outlast those who gave up too soon.

So how do you stay consistent? Here are some ideas that have proven useful to many.

Plan and pace yourself. When building new habits, don't try to do everything at once. Change is difficult. Yes, outcomes are important, but so is the process. You want to set meaningful goals, ambitious yet attainable. If your expectations are unrealistic or your task list is overwhelming, you may burn out before you can see results. If instead your goals are set too low, they will not motivate you. Or you will make little progress even if you achieve them. The key is to find the right balance.

Then develop a schedule or system to keep yourself on track. How you stay organized depends on your work style and what you're doing. You may have a simple checklist or a Gantt chart or a content calendar. The point is to make your plan explicit and actionable. Break it down into smaller steps.

Let's say you plan to contact 30 industry executives. That may sound overwhelming. Large tasks feel like they require a focused block of time. It might be weeks before you can set aside hours to do outreach. But can you make one call a day? Sure, that's doable. It lightens the mental burden of the task, and you'd finish in a month. With a clear schedule, you can visualize your task list for each day or week. You can see how they ladder up to the big picture. You can look back and celebrate your progress.

Post visible reminders. Having a schedule doesn't ensure that you will adhere to it. This is true when starting a new routine. The activity hasn't been ingrained in your mindset or muscle memory. It's easy to revert to your old habits. You may need small nudges prompting you to follow through.

While writing this book, I set a daily quota of 200 words. After a long day of work, however, I was in no mood to write. Staring at a computer screen was the last thing I wanted to do. Falling behind felt discouraging. What kept me on track was the calendar method popularized by Jerry Seinfeld. Every day I jotted down in a planner what I did, such as "organized Value sections" or "wrote the closing thoughts to Initiative." If I made any progress, I could check off that day. This motivated me to open the Word document and do *something*, even if I only had 20 minutes. Those 20 minutes added up. Now if you use this method, give yourself grace for missed days. But commit to skipping no more than once a week.

Reminders can be physical or digital, as long as they are conspicuous. Mine was a daily planner. It sat on my desk refusing to be ignored. Yours might be a recurring calendar event, an alarm that goes off at 2:30 p.m. every day, or a Post-it note on your monitor. Whatever your approach, make it visible.

Partner with other people. Changing habits can be a lonely road. We are less consistent when there's no oversight. We push back our personal deadlines. We fall behind and shrug it off. But when we must report to someone, we tend to be more responsible. So find accountability partners. Share regular updates with them.

Learn from each other's journeys. That may be the support you need to keep going.

Why is this effective? They have no formal authority over you. They aren't your boss writing you up or a professor failing you. Yet it's a powerful motivator precisely for that reason: Your partner speaks truth into your life because you've allowed them to do so. Graciously receive the critique and don't get upset at them for pushing you. If you're slacking, you must own up to it. But chances are, you're already working to be more consistent, because you don't want to let this person down.

One more thing: Whatever you do in life, there will be naysayers. Some people will think you are too young, too old, too reckless, too bold. They may voice their criticism or offer unsolicited advice. To stay the course, you must tune out the noise. Accountability partners help you to stand strong in the face of rejection; to persevere in times of great difficulty; to remain centered in the midst of doubt.

Push through the inertia. Even without active opposition, we ourselves have plenty of excuses and distractions. If you're like most people, your motivation will fluctuate. Some days you won't feel like doing the work. Of course, you should rest when needed. Don't chase consistency at the cost of your mental or physical well-being. Sometimes you just need a break or a good night's rest.

Here I'm talking about making excuses like "not feeling motivated" or "not being in the mood." That happens to all of us. Some days I don't feel inspired to write. But when I make time to do it anyway, I'm always glad that I did. Once I get into the groove, the ideas start to flow. Again, it's like working out. Despite how unmotivated I may have felt, I've never left the gym regretting that I went. There's a misconception that our feelings must drive our actions. The relationship often goes the other way.

The heart of consistency is discipline. You may do something because you feel like it. Or you do it first, and then the feelings will follow. This applies to many important things in life. Often we show kindness because we care; we act honestly because we feel a sense of morality. But sometimes we should act kind, even when we don't feel warm and fuzzy. We should maintain integrity despite being tempted to compromise. The habit builds the character and defines the priorities.

Likewise, you may work on your project only when inspiration strikes. Or you could invest time and effort every day because you truly believe in it. You may reach out and meet people only when you feel social. Or you could build relationships day in and day out—bringing value to others in your routine activities. With proper discipline, you'll find good friends, a thriving network, and new opportunities.

The best antidote for inertia is to remember your motivation. Branding consultant Mara Rada explains why she posts on LinkedIn every day: "It not only gives you reach, but also the benefit of familiarity with partners and clients." She recounts an interaction with a colleague. Even though they hadn't spoken in a year, he sees her content regularly and told her: "It feels like we're always in touch on LinkedIn."[3] Consistency keeps you in others' consciousness, even when you may not be aware of it.

Pick yourself back up. The point isn't to be consistent for its own sake. Think of any habit either personal or professional. What do you do when you fail? When you lapse on your diet? Miss a day of your gym schedule? Break your perfect attendance? Fall back into your old ways?

For many people, one slip-up leads to another. They would've done anything to prevent that first blunder. But the second one was less consequential and the third one lesser still. Their motivation had shifted from the intrinsic (pursuing the activity) to the extrinsic (maintaining their record). So when their streak was broken, their reason to be disciplined went with it.

This shouldn't be the case. Justin Earley articulates in *The Common Rule*: "The pattern, not the anomaly, is the key."[4] Cultivate habits, not legalism. Pursue growth, not streaks. Remember why you do it in the first place. Stand up and dust yourself off. Hold your head high and keep going.

We spend too much of our lives trying to avoid mistakes. When we inevitably slip, we waste even more time moping over it—or worse, jettisoning our progress. I get it. Nobody wants to fail. But life isn't about keeping a perfect record. And there is no way to mitigate all the risks.

Being consistent builds resilience in the face of adversity. When you fail, learn from it. When you fall down, get back up. The act of bouncing back from defeat or rejection is as important a muscle as any other. The more you exercise it, the stronger you will get. Failure may still hurt, but the pain will bother you less. Those who have been tested emerge with thicker skin and a stronger will.

Think of it this way: You try something once. You fail. You feel devastated, because you had prepared for so long and placed all your hope into this one opportunity.

Now let's say you make three attempts and are still unsuccessful. You may feel disappointed, but I assure you that the third time is not like the first. The third time, if you're like most people, would feel less personal. It would hold less weight, less power over you. Either you'd be motivated to do better next time, or you'd try something else. But you wouldn't waste time moping. You wouldn't feel paralyzed by defeat. You would get up and keep moving forward.

When you are consistent in your efforts, the value you offer and receive will compound. The friendships you develop will be loyal and lasting. You can let go of the pressure to excel every time. This frees you up to explore, to hold things in perspective, and ultimately to achieve more. You don't need to knock it out of the park on the first try. You just need to take more swings.

Moving up: Maintaining what matters
We cannot talk about consistency without discussing your trajectory over time. There's an inherent temporal component: a past, a present, and a future—all constantly changing as you move forward in life. Look back a year or two and see how far you've come. Look back five or 10 years, and the changes are even more dramatic. Chances are, you've made progress in your career. You've honed your skills. You've grown in your maturity and understanding of the world. You're no longer the same person.

Even if you weren't deliberate about it, you've likely experienced growth and development. That's a natural part of life. But when you consistently show up to places, follow up with people, and keep up your activities, your progress will accelerate. You will reach higher perches and greater powers.

As you move up, it's imperative to know what to change and what to continue doing. Here are mindsets and practices to hold onto as you advance—both in your career and in your organization.

In your career. It's often said that "what got you here won't get you there." Yes, but that doesn't mean that what got you here isn't valuable. Circumstances may have been less-than-ideal, but they were good enough. Perhaps they were precisely what you had needed at the time.

Many people take for granted the path behind them. They feel that they've outgrown their old lives—their upbringing, their hometowns, their experiences, their social circles. Let me illustrate.

In the Netflix movie *Always Be My Maybe*, there's a scene where the main characters are seated at a small dim sum restaurant. Sasha Tran (Ali Wong), now a celebrity chef, snobbishly comments to Marcus Kim (Randall Park) that she can't believe that restaurant was still in business. She had grown accustomed to the finer things in life. "What are we even doing here?" she asks.

Marcus responds that he eats there twice a week. Her problem, he explains, is that she has painted her whole childhood and teenage years in a negative light. She has unfairly dismissed the things of her youth—before the money and fame and success. She has forgotten her roots.[5]

We may do this in our career journeys as well. We look at our college degrees and downplay the value of our education. We look at our old jobs and only remember the bad parts. We look at our old teachers and peers and think they're unsophisticated. We look at our old professional groups and say that's just for students. We look at our old neighborhoods and shun the people who live there.

The truth is: Different parts of the journey will look different. That's to be expected when there's career advancement and social mobility. But your past is not any less valuable. That was your lot at the time. And you did what you could with what you had.

Now you may not use your degree anymore, but it helped you land your first job. You may no longer be in the same profession, but you gained valuable skills through it. You may have lost touch with certain people, but they played a part in your personal development. All good things in their own seasons.

So embrace the impermanence of life. Celebrate your present circumstances. Look ahead, work hard, and reach for your potential. But never forget where you came from. Honor what got you here.

In your organization. As you move up, people in your company will treat you differently. They will hold you to higher standards. They will scrutinize your words and actions. They will share information with you less. They will talk about you more. Former peers will distance themselves from you. Former bosses will compete with you head-on. These are some of the unwelcome changes of formal leadership.

Having been promoted, you may grow prideful and arrogant. You may let the money and power go to your head. You may develop an inflated ego or adopt a larger-than-life persona. You may start looking down on others. Fight these common temptations. Wherever you are in your career, continue to treat people with dignity. Being out of touch is the quickest way to lose respect, influence, and friends.

A colleague shared this story that serves as a good visual analogy. She used to work at a large institution in New York City. The elevator was packed as people were returning from lunch. A couple executives and board members entered. They were heading to a meeting at the top. On the way up, she heard them grumbling that the elevator stopped so many times for people to get off. Imagine being so privileged that you get upset because the common folk need to go back to work.

Remember to stay humble. The higher you go in the organization, the more you must rely on other people to get things done. Relationships are essential to your career ascent. They are even more important when you're at the top. Stay rooted by getting to know people at all levels.

As you rise, you will start to lose sight of the ground. You will increasingly deal with vision and strategy, rather than details and operations. You will depend on layers of management to carry out your mission. Those layers will filter the information you receive. In part, this is necessary so you aren't overwhelmed by a million requests. Your direct reports will let you know what requires your attention.

Yet they may also filter out crucial information. They may be afraid to escalate issues or share bad news with you.[6] They may present skewed data and rosy pictures to make themselves look good. They may not be completely honest with you when you have a bad idea. As a leader, your job is to make timely, appropriate decisions. So delays in getting the right information will dampen your efficacy.

Now I'm not telling you to distrust your people or circumvent them. I'm just encouraging you to seek out and listen to perspectives from beyond your team. You can learn so much from people up and down in the organization. Executives may share about potential strategic directions. Middle managers may shed light on current market pressures. Frontline staff may tell you about the problems they face and the workarounds they use. This helps you keep a pulse on the company. It puts things into context.

Moreover, find people who are comfortable telling you the truth, calling you out on your blind spots, and pushing back on your half-baked ideas. They may be your executive assistant or chief of staff; a previous boss or an internal mentor; your peers and former peers. Or they may come from unexpected places in the organization. These relationships will be essential to your success.

Beyond gaining information, knowing your people is just good leadership. I first witnessed this when I visited Joe Avelino, CEO of a community hospital. As we walked through his facility,

Joe chatted with the receptionist. He greeted the workers in the hallway. He stopped and spoke with a janitor. Joe knew them by name. He showed interest in their lives and asked about their families. To be clear, he wasn't trying to impress anyone. There were no cameras or publicists around. This was just another day.

Unfortunately, that kind of leadership is the exception and not the norm. Many employees today feel unappreciated, invisible, even disposable. They've been treated like a number or a cog in the machine. Modern workplaces are impersonal. Mass layoffs are increasingly frequent. And morale is down across industries. It's no wonder that employees struggle to find meaning and belonging.

What would it look like to defy the trends? To know and honor each individual, regardless of their rank? Would it improve employee morale, creativity, and performance? Would it change the atmosphere of the workplace? Would it drive superior company results? All these outcomes are possible. But they won't occur overnight. As a leader, you must model the behaviors you wish to see. Manifest the culture you desire. Demonstrate it by your words and actions. Be consistent and others will follow.

CLOSING THOUGHTS

We began this chapter comparing networking to exercise. To extend the analogy: Suppose you want to lose weight, yet you continue to eat calorie-dense foods and drink alcohol to excess. Even if you work out four days a week, don't expect great results. It doesn't take a personal trainer to spot the problem. Your diet sabotages your gym routine. Your actions are inconsistent with your goals.

Improving your health requires not only working out but also eating well, sleeping on time, and so on. Do your lifestyle choices point in the same direction? In grad school, my housemate Kiet Ly encouraged me to start going to the gym. He showed me his workouts and taught me about nutrition. Kiet was disciplined in his intake of protein and carbs. His diet consisted of brown rice, chicken breast, veggies, and protein shakes. Sometimes he would eat a block of tofu with a spoon—that's dedication!

Likewise, networking is not isolated from the rest of your life. Building relationships requires as much an investment in yourself as it does in other people. This is a lifelong journey. How committed are you to your values? How congruent are you in your identity? As they say, we are what we repeatedly do. So live beyond reproach. Give and connect daily. Choose a lifestyle of service over random good deeds. Your habits will take shape with practice. Your reputation will stem from consistency.

* * *

We've covered a lot of information. So before moving on, let's review. We've discussed three of the five elements: value, initiative, and consistency. These lay the foundation for your networking efforts.

- Value: You know who you are and what you can offer. You hold a mindset of helping others without expecting repayment. You notice their needs and connect them with solutions.
- Initiative: Not only are you observant and well-prepared, but you also reach out. You don't wait for life to happen; you set things in motion. You create opportunities for yourself and others.
- Consistency: You do it not just once, or now and then, but regularly. Your actions become habits. After meeting

people, you follow up. You keep in touch to nurture the relationship.

With that mindset of giving value, taking initiative and being consistent, you have the basics down. I know that you will meet a lot of people. You will move ahead in your career and your life. You are an avid networker now, you might say. After all, you're doing more than most people.

But I don't think you'd want to stop there—not when there are two more elements to take your networking to the next level. To deepen and enrich your relationships. To draw people to you and not always be the one initiating. To add heart to your networking. These are Relatability and Credibility. They are in part about empathy, in part about expertise. We now turn our attention to these elements.

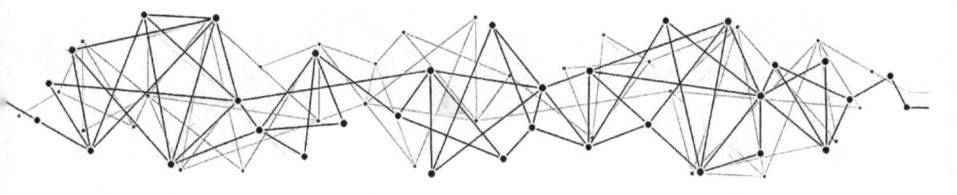

Element 4:

RELATABILITY

I have a confession to make: In my earlier jobs, I wasn't close with my coworkers at all.

Sure, we got along. We worked well together. We were cordial but not close. We were friendly but not friends. Our knowledge of one another was surface-level: He's into basketball. She likes the color purple. They are militant vegans. The sort of things you observe or soon learn after meeting someone. We may have remembered a fun fact about each other. But that was the extent of it.

I didn't engage in much small talk either. Though we shared about our weekends, the chitchat was kept to a minimum. We mostly talked shop. That was efficient for getting work done but not effective for making friends. We seldom spent time together outside the office. Even at company lunches, where people let loose, I had work on my mind. In hindsight, I wasn't that fun to be around.

In contrast, I noticed that the leaders would do life together. They knew one another's spouses and kids. They invited each other over for dinner. They went on weekend outings. They talked about their families and national issues and everything in between. They honestly seemed close with one another. These observations taught me a crucial lesson: Work relationships are not just about work.

To be fair, my coworkers were much older than I was. I didn't watch the shows they watched. I didn't have kids' soccer games to attend. I didn't yet deal with adult issues like taxes and politics.

But here's the thing: Despite all the rhetoric around age or generational differences—or any other characteristic—we are much more alike than different. If you're reading this book, you have things in common with other readers. We share universal motivations. We all want to improve our personal and professional lives. And we understand that, to be successful, we must build solid relationships.

This chapter focuses on being relatable. Relatability is not a matter of pretense or posturing. It requires effort and intentionality. You must take a genuine interest in others, spend time to learn about them, and find authentic points of connection. Let us begin with a brief survey of the human psyche.

A common desire for dignity

Not everyone craves fame. Not everyone chases fortune. But everyone I've met—from young to old, across races and religions—has wanted, expected, even fought for one fundamental thing: dignity. We want to be treated with respect. We want to be known, to feel seen and heard. We want our presence to be valued, our absence to be noticed, our existence to matter.

To relate with others, show them respect. Make people feel valued, and you will be received with open arms. But hurt their pride or make them feel unimportant, and you will trigger a fight-or-flight response. Either they will put up their defenses, or they will avoid you altogether. Neither is conducive to your relationship. See, not everyone has a big ego, but we all have an instinct for self-preservation.

We want to be viewed in a positive light. We're frustrated when people underestimate us. We set out to prove ourselves in their eyes ("I'll show you!"). Or we lament the lack of opportunity to do so ("If only I had a chance"). Yet when they overestimate us, we also feel burdened by their expectations and undeserving of their praise. The sweet spot seems to be a slight overestimation.

We want others to believe in us—perhaps a bit more than we believe in ourselves. If it's just enough of a stretch, we would rise to the occasion. We would grow into the role. David Brooks explains: "There is something in being seen that brings forth growth. If you beam the light of your attention on me, I blossom. If you see great potential in me, I will probably come to see great potential in myself."[1]

In social situations, we want to either fit in or stand out. Often it's a mix of both. We long to join groups we deem desirable. To rub shoulders with those who are smart and successful. To sit with the cool kids. In many professions, pride is found in belonging to a guild or tradition: This is what it means to be a doctor, a scientist, a judge, or a general. But even in those groups, we may aspire to stand out. As we progress in our careers, we may want to be admired and esteemed among our peers.

Now some people are more career-oriented than others. Some have greater ambitions and appetites for risk. Some take a longer view or a more global perspective. Your definition of success likely differs from mine, according to our values, abilities, inclinations, and circumstances. But we all have duties and dreams, things that we work for and work toward. And we want to be successful in them.

In every season and across walks of life, one theme rings constant: We want to matter. We want our time and talents to make a difference. We feel validated by our successes, whether that means leaving a public legacy or simply providing for our families. Through the work of our hands, we find dignity. That said, we are more than our professions, our performance, or our potential.

We are more than our jobs

When it comes to networking, there tends to be an overemphasis on work. Many people view others in terms of titles and credentials. This reflects a mindset of transactional value and reinforces a culture of "What can you do for me?" That's not how we want to approach networking.

It's ineffective because it fails to honor the individual. It treats people as caricatures or a list of static attributes. It makes broad assumptions about them based on those traits: that they share the beliefs common in their profession; that they represent the values of their employer; and so on. These assumptions are not always true. In fact, such premature conclusions may be growing less accurate.

Consider a few recent trends: First, our workplaces are becoming less homogenous due to demographic shifts, economic pressures, and inclusion initiatives. Fields historically dominated by one group are seeing interest from others. More women are entering tech. More men are going into nursing. More ethnic minorities are pursuing careers in finance. There's just more diversity. As people bring different lived experiences to the workplace, assumptions based on profession may miss the mark.

Second, people are changing jobs more frequently than in past decades, whether by choice or by consequence. Gone are the days of spending one's entire career at a single employer. That is now rare outside of academia. Today's business environment is faster-paced, more competitive, and more volatile. Layoffs are not uncommon. Employees leave for quicker advancement. And many people explore new careers during economic downturns. Whatever the case, our jobs are not permanent.

Third, opportunities abound today for remote work and entrepreneurship. Some find gig work through two-sided marketplaces. Others perform freelance services or take on fractional leadership roles. Still others create content, open e-commerce stores, or develop their own apps. These pursuits may lead to full-time businesses. Indeed, many employees are building their personal brands and side hustles to escape the nine-to-five. Therefore, it's foolish to typecast people based on their day jobs.

It's also a mistake to treat them as a proxy for their employer online. Social media is, first and foremost, social. We represent ourselves as individuals. People want to connect with other people, not companies. Relationships contingent on one's position or employer may, without warning, fall into question. People switch jobs, change careers, and retire. They get promoted, moved, or let go. Change is inevitable. When it does happen, you don't want it to sever your ties and negate your efforts.

But relationships grounded in something deeper will outlast the transitions. People will think of you when they move onto new roles. They may invite you to come work with them. They may share valuable information with you. They may select your company as a vendor or a strategic partner.

To be clear, I'm not advising you to avoid talking about work. That's where the conversation may start. It's often the basis for your initial contact. And you can certainly relate with others through talking shop, sharing best practices, or even discussing industrywide problems.

I'm saying you shouldn't *only* talk about work. Recall my intro vignette. Building relationships feels more natural when you find connection beyond your jobs. It's more effective as well. Let's say you both work in retail pharmacy. Sure, you can bond over work. You can commiserate over staffing issues or opine on the direction of the field. Those conversations aren't unique though. Your companion likely knows many people in pharmacy, as do you. If all you talk about is work, you'll be unmemorable.

But if you also bond over a hobby, for example, you will stand out. Whether you share a love of surfing or winemaking, Scrabble or pigeon-racing, a mutual interest helps to break the ice. The more uncommon it is, the more immediate the bond. It may be a reason to keep in touch as well.

Now you can't force or fake relating with others. The goal isn't to be a walking encyclopedia with a million icebreaker topics. The goal is to live an examined life, doing the things you're interested in and passionate about. Any bond should come as a natural byproduct of living with intention.

I stumbled upon this gem of a quote. Published in 1915, it still rings true, perhaps even truer, today: "Live an active life among people who are doing worthwhile things, keep eyes and ears and mind and heart open to absorb truth, and then tell of the things you know, as if you know them. The world will listen, for the world loves nothing so much as real life."[2]

So go out in wonder. Explore new horizons. Do worthwhile things. For the most compelling stories come from the stuff of real life. Not concepts but examples. Not hypotheticals but history. Not generalities but specifics. Not airbrushed but unfiltered, imperfect, messy as life may be.

Then speak from your lived experience. Tell of the paths you've walked, the people you've met, the moments you've committed to memory. Share what you did, what you said, and how you felt. As you do so, you will meet others who can relate. You will find yourself in the company of friends.

Researchers say it takes 50 hours together for acquaintances to become casual friends, 90 more hours to grow into good friends, and over 200 hours to consider each other confidants.[3] These are rough estimates, but directionally they make sense. Developing a bond requires spending time and experiencing life together. That said, quality of time matters more than quantity. You can become friends more quickly when you see each other as real people with lives outside of work.

Ultimately, people are not one-dimensional. To get to know someone, relate with the individual, not the position. Connect on a more personal level than job responsibilities. Let's dive deeper.

Finding points of commonality

Here's the heart of the matter: We are all human. We have passions and interests, hopes and dreams, fears and insecurities. Each of us plays various roles in our lives. You may be a husband and a father, a son and a brother, a friend and a colleague, an employee and a boss. And that may not even cover half of your social identities. Some are even more salient. We identify ourselves by our race, ethnicity, and country of origin; our religious and political affiliation; our sexual orientation and gender identity; even our socioeconomic status and the community in which we live. All these traits shape who we are.

To initiate or deepen a relationship, find things in common—reasons to talk and do life together. If you have a scheduled meeting, take time to learn about the person beforehand. Look at their LinkedIn profile, website, or blog. It's easy to find public information about people these days. If it's a chance encounter, there's more of an art to eliciting responses and keeping the conversation going.

Think of it this way: Relatability means getting to know someone and letting yourself be known at the same time. Both parts are necessary, and many people struggle with one or the other.

You can't shortcut the process. "We may achieve familiarity while wearing our masks," John White explains, "That is why spurious attempts at intimacy on a first name basis or on casual embraces at a cocktail party prove unsatisfying and boring." He goes on: "And since we only see what we want to see, and expose nothing but the image we want to project, we enter an alliance of mutual contempt."[4]

But when we look beyond ourselves and our own interests, when we invest the time and energy to see—indeed, to behold—the people around us, we will achieve more than familiarity. We will know and be known.

You may need to show more interest in those around you. Or you may need to be less guarded about yourself. In either case, listen more than you speak and ask good follow-up questions. This helps to build rapport—remember what we said about reciprocity—and it gives you a base of knowledge to work from.

Then draw the connections as soon as possible. Perhaps you attended the same college. You can reminisce about your campus experiences. Or you used to live in the same town. You can bond over your favorite places and pastimes there. Sharing memories helps to break the ice.

Don't be afraid to incorporate other aspects of yourself into your narrative—subjects that tie in naturally and may spark further dialogue. Let's examine three key categories. Strong bonds can often be found in shared experiences, common interests, and mutual connections.

Shared experiences. People are more likely to support you if they can relate to you. And there's no more profound commonality than having walked in each other's shoes.

We began this section talking about our roles and salient identities. Take a moment and think about the top three or four ways you identify. They can be as general or as specific as you'd like. They can describe the present or be somewhat aspirational. They can include your profession but shouldn't be limited to it. These tend to be the core attributes that frame how you view and approach life.

For example, I identify as a Protestant Christian, a Vietnamese American, a relationship builder, and a healthcare leader. Of course, I have many other traits, roles, and affiliations. All of us do. But these are most foundational to who I am today. Whether I had chosen or inherited these characteristics, they inform my personal values and perspectives. They shape my daily experiences and priorities.

How do you identify? Which dimensions matter most to your sense of self? What do you hold sacred? Some people view themselves in terms of their political or religious beliefs. Others identify most with their cultural heritage or sexual orientation. Still others are eager to make known their role as a parent, their status as a veteran, or their lifestyle as a vegetarian. Who do you say you are?

When you meet people who share these identities, try to connect on a deeper level. How that appears depends on the context. At a public event, it may mean having a lively conversation with knowing looks and mutual affirmations. Over a meal together, it may mean opening up about personal struggles and ambitions, hopes and fears, even trials and tragedies. There are moments in life when the greatest comfort is to be with another person who understands, who has walked the same road.

Keith Ferrazzi, former chief marketing officer at Deloitte, says that out of the many ways we can help others, three domains stand above the rest: health, wealth, and children. "When you help someone through a health issue, positively impact someone's personal wealth, or take a sincere interest in their children, you engender life-bonding loyalty."[5] I would expand on this statement. Beyond what you can do *for* them, the true value is in being *with* them. To celebrate in their joy. To share in their sorrow. To walk parallel paths through rough, uncertain terrain. To relate together as you both navigate a medical diagnosis, financial troubles, or parenting challenges. These experiences forge the strongest bonds.

Lean into your shared experiences: the immigrant experience, the working mother experience, the young leader experience, and so on. As you see, these don't need to be rare. Your experiences don't need to be identical either. They just need to have affected your lives in similar, significant ways.

A special bond may form, however, when your shared experience involves being a minority in a profession or industry: Women in engineering. Men in teaching. Black people in technology. Southeast Asians in leadership. Christians in the arts. Republicans in health policy. Older people in advertising. Veterans in the civilian workforce. You get the idea. These may one day change, but at the time of writing, they are all stark examples of minorities in their respective fields. It's lonely being the only one, so relationships may form more quickly when people meet another like themselves.

Now I called this section shared experiences, not characteristics, for a reason. Many people may check the same box on a demographic survey. However, their lived experiences may be irreconcilably different. They may share an ethnic background, but some are first generation while others had parents and grandparents born in this country. Likewise, they may profess the same faith, yet some are devotees while others are dabblers. What's creed to one person is cherry-picked by another.

So you can't assume based on first impressions. Noticing similarities is a starting point, and people can certainly relate to you based on the trait itself. But trust takes root more deeply where there are shared lived experiences. Rapport is found in the personal stories. There's familiarity in the details, human connection in the me-too. These are uncovered only through conversation.

Common interests. Another approach is to relate over the things you both like. These can range from casual hobbies to personal passions and everything in between: the books you read, the movies you watch, the bands you listen to, the sports you follow, the activities you enjoy, the causes you support, and so much more. All of these are fair game. There's no limit to what you can discuss.

Find subjects that you're both excited about, things you can discuss in depth and at length. You'd avoid any awkward silence or forced chatter, especially if you had just met. It certainly beats talking about the weather.

The key is to be observant. Pay attention to what people wear or carry with them; it may indicate that they identify with a certain brand, activity, or fandom. Listen to what they say, including details they mention in passing. Hone in on a topic you can talk about: "So you said you're into snowboarding?" or "I also do yoga on the weekends."

Notice also what they display in their office or what's behind them in a video call. Whenever I see a musical instrument or a movie poster or a Funko Pop figurine I recognize, I'd ask about it. Likewise, I have a chess trophy and a Pokéball on my shelf. It's amazing how many conversations those have sparked. Yes, it may sound silly to bond over board games and TV shows. But there's nothing trivial about finding common ground and being well liked.

On the wrong subjects, you won't connect at all. The dialogue will be dry, and then you'll each go your way. But with a common interest, the conversation will be enjoyable. It will feel natural. You will build rapport and perhaps make a new friend. Think about a time you had geeked out over a topic with someone. There's a certain camaraderie there. That's what you want.

To be clear, this is not about making small talk. See, small talk is polite chitchat about trivial matters. There's a use for it, but many people would rather watch paint dry. Instead, when you talk about a common interest, you are both engaged in the conversation. You're not just filling time. You're on the same wavelength sharing stories, exchanging ideas, and relating with one another.

Hobbies and passions can form bridges between very different people. Whereas a shared experience reflects our core identities and apparent similarities, a common interest can unite us who, on the surface, look nothing alike. Favorite sports teams, media franchises, and leisure activities can lead to unlikely friendships. They cut across the dividing lines of age and economics, race and religion. So be careful not to stereotype others based on appearance. You may have more in common than you think. Two experiences solidified this idea for me.

First, one of my hobbies in high school was recording music. At the time, there was a popular website called AcidPlanet where I met other musicians. Some were professional audio engineers, but most were enthusiasts like me. We journeyed together. We collaborated on projects. We shared tips and learned from one another.

Through the forum, I became friends with a man named Glenn Sell. I admired his piano and strings compositions. He gave me great feedback and advice as I started out. He even mailed me recording software, virtual instruments, and audio loops to use. I was touched by his care and generosity.

Now Glenn wasn't a professional music producer. He was a construction worker by trade. He was much older than me, he lived halfway across the country, and his political views were more conservative than mine. Had we met under other circumstances, there would've been little reason for us to interact, much less be friends. But there we related over our love for making music. We bonded over a common interest.

A second experience occurred in college. I was walking along ring road at UC Irvine when I spotted someone I knew. Jim McKinney, or Pastor Jim as we called him, was an older campus missionary with a gentle, grandpa-like demeanor. He was there tabling with his students. So I stopped by to say hi.

Five minutes later, a guy named Kiet Le approached us. He and I had attended the same high school, so I thought it was because he saw me. As it turned out, he and Pastor Jim knew each other. I was surprised. Kiet was an atheist who had shown little interest in spirituality. What was he doing with an evangelist? I soon learned that they went bike-riding together through a local cycling club.

Again, here were two people with differing traits and contrasting belief systems. Yet they were united by a shared activity and—here's the most important part—became invested in each other as individuals. Kiet came by to see how Jim was doing. Jim asked

Kiet about his next DJing gig. Finding commonality is the starting point for a connection, not where the relationship must remain.

Mutual connections. You may also know some of the same people, especially if you've worked in the same industry or lived in the same city. Those relationships can help you open doors with others.

"How do you know so-and-so?" we might ask. This tends to be a good icebreaker topic. Social media makes it easy to view our mutual contacts. Here's where we see the personal and professional converge. Your coworker might've been their childhood friend, their college roommate, or the best man at their wedding. Their colleague might be your friend from church, your next-door neighbor, or even your relative. In my experience, we're more interconnected than many of us realize.

Of course, having a mutual friend doesn't guarantee that you two will become friends. But it may crack that door open just a bit wider. Think of the saying: Any friend of his (or hers) is a friend of mine. As we had discussed, people tend to surround themselves with similar peers. We are known by the company we keep. So if you both hold that friend in high regard, you may warm up to each other more quickly. Through that exchange, you may uncover shared experiences or common interests too.

Taking it a step further, you may be introduced to someone or referred for a job. There is power in that connection. You come in not as a complete stranger but with some affinity, some social capital conferred by your mutual colleague. This has real, concrete implications.

My friend JC Ruffalo is an investor at Cove Fund. Whenever he shares about a startup, I'm inclined to learn more. I may meet with the founder, even if the business idea doesn't appeal to me. That's because I trust JC's judgment. If he sees something special there, then it's certainly worth a conversation.

Likewise, when people view you through a positive lens, when they expect you to be confident and charming—perhaps reflecting the traits of your mutual contact—they will look for clues that confirm their beliefs. They will interpret your words, actions, even mistakes with more grace. They will treat you in ways that put you at ease to show your best side. In this respect, perception breeds reality.

Finding points of commonality—through shared experiences, common interests, or mutual connections—generates goodwill. It predisposes people to liking you because they see you as someone like them.

Engendering warmth

Commonalities offer immediate reasons to bond, but they are not the be-alls and end-alls. Just because you have similar interests, or you know the same people, doesn't mean that you will get along.

Two individuals can look like an ideal match on paper. Yet they may meet and want nothing to do with each other. This is as true in networking as it is in dating or hiring. Chemistry isn't guaranteed by similar backgrounds. Rapport isn't ensured by shared goals and aspirations. In the end, your likeability comes from how you carry yourself and how you treat others. It's in the way you approach life.

Adopt a posture of kindness, humility, and grace. Do this, and you'll be welcomed anywhere.

Embrace kindness. I've heard it said of one workplace: "Everyone here is smart. Differentiate yourself by being kind." Many people only look out for themselves, their projects, their image, their next promotion. You need not follow the crowd. Those who are kind stand out in our dog-eat-dog world.

Kindness is countercultural. It focuses not on the self but on the good of others. It embodies a positive spirit and expresses genuine empathy. It involves helpfulness but goes beyond "random acts of kindness" or polite conduct. True kindness is rooted in strength and confidence. It is not weak or insecure. Nor does it yield to that which is wrong. Above all, it requires a choice—hence the need to *embrace* being kind.

One expression is in the way we speak. In a culture that tears people down, be the one to build them up. Refrain from the watercooler gossip. Don't criticize, complain, or condemn. Instead, use your words to encourage and affirm others. Speak well of them in their absence.

Similarly, introduce them with honor. Praise them in public. I worked with a sales leader who did this masterfully. He talked people up in front of the company. He made them look good to clients and partners. It's no wonder they liked him. Yet the effect doesn't end with those who are commended.

When you speak well of people, listeners will take note. Those around will see that you are different—secure in your identity and truly concerned about others. You will be known as a kind person, a supportive colleague, a positive influence, a loyal friend. You are someone worth associating with.

Exhibit humility. Another admirable trait is humility. Not false modesty or humble-bragging, which only draws attention to oneself. True humility, like kindness, is grounded in self-awareness and quiet confidence. Humble people don't feel the need to always be the leader or expert in the room. They have no problem saying, "I don't know." They hold strong opinions but readily admit when they were wrong. They understand that no man or woman is an island, and they give credit where it is due.

My friend Nick Carranza exemplifies this. He knows exactly who he is and who he's not. Nick grew up in a rough neighborhood. His future didn't look too bright. Yet because one teacher believed in him, Nick learned to believe in himself. He became a photographer and producer working with big names in politics, healthcare, and entertainment. A lesser man might boast about pulling himself up by his bootstraps. But Nick recognizes and attributes his success to the power of mentorship.

When Nick presented to my UCLA students, he was voted the best guest speaker of the quarter. It wasn't because he had the most impressive credentials or the biggest personality. He didn't. But he was the most relatable. His story resonated with them. His humility and authenticity were magnetic.

Moreover, he engaged the students. He asked questions. He was genuinely curious about each student and what motivated them. Curiosity comes from the Latin *curiositas*, which is traced back to the root word *cura* meaning care. When we express curiosity, we show that we care about other people. We care to learn who they are. We care to hear their thoughts and feelings. This can take some humility. As it is said, humility isn't thinking less of yourself, it's thinking of yourself less—and others more.

Extend grace. Sometimes we encounter people who irritate us. They make hurtful assumptions and unkind remarks. They do careless things that cause us trouble. It may be easy to lose our temper.

Consider showing grace instead. Hold your tongue. Unclench your fists. Let it go. Grace is about patience and forgiveness, approaching life with a gentler spirit. A harsh response may feel good in the moment, but it does nothing positive. It only stokes the fire and pushes onlookers away. People may not even know they had offended you. So be quick to listen and slow to judge. Assume positive intent.

People aren't perfect. They make mistakes and things go wrong. Assume positive intent. Was it out of negligence, or would you have done the same thing in those circumstances? Hindsight is 20/20.

People may say mean and disrespectful things. Assume positive intent. Do their words come from a place of ignorance or malice? Though the former doesn't excuse what they said, it is different. Ignorance can be corrected, and tact can be taught. The roots of ill will, however, tend to run deep.

And other times, people may say things that infuriate you. Yet in a calmer state of mind, you realize that you had overreacted. Perhaps you were stressed and on edge. It's especially easy to read hostility into text where no such negativity was intended or present. Assume positive intent. Is the issue with their delivery, or is it in your perception? After all, communication is a two-way street.

Let me be clear: Assuming positive intent doesn't mean believing that everyone you meet has your best interest in mind. That would be naïve. But it does mean pausing to consider how you respond to life. It means checking your gut reactions, withholding judgment, and showing grace.

By assuming positive intent, we can avoid misunderstandings. We create space for relationships. We make our corner of the world that much warmer and gentler. We become likeable, relatable people.

When we act with kindness, humility, and grace, we will naturally stand out. Others will want to know us. They may emulate those characteristics to relate with us. Isn't that a vision worth manifesting?

Employing humor

Another powerful device in your relational toolkit is humor. Shared laughter is both a sign and a catalyst of relatability. Being playful shows that you are comfortable with one another. And joking together builds goodwill.

While it comes in many forms, here we'll discuss conversational humor. This may include telling prepared jokes and funny stories. But more often, the jokes are impromptu: casual banter, comedic observations, clever wordplays, and so on. Instead of answering a question literally, you could throw in a playful twist. Whatever the form, consider both your content and delivery. Here are a few pointers.

Content. Know your audience. Jokes may be funny to one group but not to another. After all, people must understand what you're talking about to get why it's humorous. Does your joke rely on specific knowledge? Does it require shared values and beliefs? Some jokes have mass appeal; most people can relate to them through general experience. Others require additional context. An obscure reference may make sense to just a couple people. A brilliant pun may be appreciated by only a few.

Test your jokes. Tell them in various settings, and see how people react. You may want to start with your friends. Not every joke will land every time—and that's the point. By testing them, you'll soon have an idea of what works and what doesn't. Hold onto the ones that consistently gets laughs.

Some jokes poke fun at people. Teasing each other can be a playful way to bond. However, you want to consider the relationship. How well do you know this person? Would he or she take it in good humor, even dishing it back? It's one thing to make fun of your siblings or close friends. You have history together, and they know your intentions. But those same remarks may be inappropriate to someone you just met.

In general, it's better to laugh with your companion, not at their expense. If you do tease them, target quirky behaviors, rather than personal attributes—especially ones they cannot change. Keep it light; avoid possible insecurities and struggles. And if they seem uncomfortable, back off immediately. You don't want to offend anyone or trample their boundaries. Apologize if you were out of line.

Often it's better to make fun of yourself, and allow others to relate to it. There are common experiences we can find amusement in together. Being able to laugh at yourself shows confidence. That said, joke about things that don't trigger your insecurities or put yourself down.

It's also a good idea to avoid sensitive, risqué, or dark topics. Don't be overly negative either. Much of what passes for humor these days is merely contempt for another group—jabs at their misfortune. It may be funny once or twice, but ongoing negativity is fatiguing. You are better than that. Learn to be an impartial judge of your own jokes. Likewise, read the room. Recognize when it's not the right time to lighten the mood. Exercise the wisdom and discipline to self-filter—before someone else calls you out.

Delivery. In college, I took a criminology class called Interrogations and Confessions. One guest speaker was a seasoned prosecutor. He completely changed the way I thought about presentations. "It's not the words, it's the music," he told us. The power is in the delivery—the context, the buildup, the emotions.

This applies to humor as well. Two people can tell the same joke and get vastly different responses. Why? Because delivery matters. The way you tell a joke can either augment or diminish its comedic nature. If you nail the delivery, people may be roaring with laughter. But if you mumble it matter-of-factly, the joke will fall flat. Set the stage with the energy you want.

Consider your tone and facial expression. A playful smile and a lively voice suggest that you're about to say something lighthearted. Others will mirror your sense of joy, which will subtly cheer you on. Speak confidently through your smile, as if you could not contain your amusement. You might even laugh as you tell the joke. In fact, if you find it hilarious, you won't need to remember these tips. It will come out that way naturally.

My friend Emma Hills has a go-to joke: "What does a nosy pepper do? It gets *jalapeño business!*" I've heard this several times now. All our mutual friends have too. We know exactly what she will say. But everyone still laughs each time she tells it. Mind you, it's not even an original joke. What makes it funny is her delivery. She imbues it with her charm. A smile on her lips, a twinkle in her eye, a playful tone and pause for anticipation—there's perfect congruence in her delivery. She herself finds such amusement in telling it, and she takes us along for the ride.

Perhaps you're not one to tell jokes, but we all have amusing stories to share now and then. Here's how you can be more engaging. First, tell stories in the present tense. Bring the audience into the action with you. Let them feel the emotional twists and turns. Second, embody the characters. Act out the scene with voices and gestures. Don't worry about looking goofy; that's part of the bit. Third, be concise. Avoid tangents and superfluous facts. You have the whole scene playing in your head because you experienced it. But your listeners are piecing the picture together as you go. So stay focused. Not every detail is necessary. Slow down and press into the ones that matter. Lastly, there's the setup. You can indicate that you're about to tell a funny story: "So this one time…" or "A funny thing happened…"

Don't worry if it feels unnatural at first. Humor is a break from our usual linear and literal thinking. Like anything else, it takes practice. Let yourself be creative, even to feel silly. When you find what works, stick with it.

Ultimately, the goal isn't to become a comedian. You don't need to tell the wittiest jokes or to get the biggest laughs. You simply want to be a cheerful, good-natured person, someone people enjoy being around. So bring a positive spirit. Laugh at others' jokes. Chime in and play along.

Relating in community

So far we've talked about meeting people "out there." A chance encounter at an event. Direct outreach to someone in the industry. Meeting people in general, regardless of context.

Most of our relationships, however, come from the groups and settings that we're already in: workers on the same team, members of the same club. Commonalities lead us into community. Into something bigger than ourselves. Into relationships with people doing things that are relevant to us.

First, let's talk about the workplace. People often think of networking as an external activity. But your workplace shouldn't be overlooked. In a traditional full-time job, you spend half your waking hours with coworkers. So make an effort to know them. It's easier to connect than if you were an outsider. I've found that most coworkers would respond positively, even if you're from different departments.

Beyond the workplace, get involved in your professional associations. They foster a sense of belonging that motivates members to help each other. I first experienced this when I joined the American College of Healthcare Executives (ACHE), which I mentioned previously. Through this group, I met hospital VPs and CEOs. As a grad student, I wouldn't have known them even had I worked at their organizations. Yet at ACHE meetings, they came up to me and asked how I was doing. They remembered me from prior events. I had their personal cell phone numbers. To a 22-year-old student, that was wild. It taught me the power of being on the same team, of relating as part of the same community.

This idea is not limited to professional settings. Find connections through your church, political party, volunteer group, or neighborhood association. Some communities involve formal, paid memberships; others are by proximity or self-identification. If you're a student, get involved in a few campus groups. Exercise those muscles early, so you'll feel comfortable relating in various contexts.

In particular, look for groups at the intersection of your interests and identities. There you may find deeper bonds as you can relate across multiple dimensions. Let me share two personal examples.

One was the Association of Asian Healthcare Leaders (AAHL). Though there were societies for Black and Hispanic healthcare administrators, one did not exist for Asian Americans. So Eddie Lai founded AAHL to fill that gap. As the group gained traction, he invited me to serve as the inaugural chair of mentorship. This united my experiences in healthcare and career advising with my Asian heritage.

Another was the Faith Driven Investor community. It's a movement that teaches Christians to be good stewards in deploying capital for global impact. When Mark Washington announced that he was hosting a cohort, I immediately signed up. I knew Mark from InterVarsity's MBA ministry. The Faith Driven Investor group combined my interest in venture capital with my identity as a follower of Jesus.

Now to relate with others in a community, you must share their goals, values, and beliefs. You must do the things they do. This may sound obvious, but it's worth calling out. Some people join a group just to promote themselves, to push their products, or to put it on their resume. They want the contacts and benefits of affiliation. Yet they don't contribute to the group. They don't participate in the life of the community. They don't do the real work involved in building relationships.

Ask yourself: Do you want to be a part of this community, or do you just want something from them? If your answer is the latter, find another approach. You can meet those people elsewhere. Otherwise, you must act in ways that are not true to who you are. With such incongruence, it's difficult to relate freely. You can't fake your way in or keep up the charades over time.

In one mission-driven organization, the new president drew the line with employees: "If this is what you believe, then we want you to stay. If not, then you have come here under false pretenses, and you must go."[6] That may sound harsh, but it's likely best for all involved. Go where you're proud to be.

Then celebrate the work of your community. Talk about its events, activities, and impact. Lift people up and highlight their contributions. Use your social media to acknowledge and advocate for the group. We had discussed this idea on an individual level. It's even more powerful in the context of a community. Branding expert Vince Parry explains that people align with brands that are "a flattering self-reflection" of their values. They are drawn to those things in which they can see themselves.[7]

Even when sharing your own journey or achievement, make it about more than just yourself. Thank community members who had inspired, mentored, or supported you. Give a shoutout to those you've learned from. Invite others into your story—to consider your takeaways or to share their own.

When you shine the light onto yourself, it only appeals to your sphere of influence. But when you direct the spotlight onto the community, it would attract the group's members and supporters. Some may not know who you are. But because of their affiliation with the group, they would applaud and engage with what you say. In this way, there's a halo effect casting a positive light on you as well.

That said, don't talk about a group all the time. Practice moderation. To be relatable, you must retain your identity apart from the group. You don't want to come across as the company's mouthpiece or the community's fanboy or fangirl. If you do so, you would gain the support of that group's members but alienate outsiders. You would erode your opportunities to relate with others.

To be clear, engaging in community should lead to direct relationships. We don't relate with corporate bodies as a whole. We relate with people one-on-one. You may be part of the same school, church, company, or association. You may see each other in passing. But shaking hands and exchanging hellos don't constitute much of a relationship. Take the time to know people individually.

Finally, when you need help or advice, ask people one-on-one. Don't rely on broadcasting to the group. You want to avoid two common problems here: The first is the bystander effect. When people see that you asked 50 others, each will assume that somebody else will help. In the end, perhaps no one does. The second is groupthink. In a communal setting, people tend to give trite, popular responses. But in private, the answers you receive will be more honest, nuanced, and personal—that is, more valuable.

Using discernment

As we close this chapter, I'd like to offer a few words of caution. These are informed by common pitfalls when people try too hard to be relatable. It feels contrived, disingenuous, and uncomfortable for everyone. That's the image of networking that people despise. You don't want to be that guy or gal. Relating with others should feel natural. You can set the stage, but you can't force it to happen.

Most of these errors are a matter of degree—taking a good thing too far or too fast. What's welcome with one person may be a nonstarter with another. Consider the nature of your relationship. Practice discernment in your interactions. Be self-aware and disciplined in your conduct. Here are several guidelines to keep you on course.

First, developing a relationship takes time. On rare occasions, you may click with someone and become instant besties. But it's usually a gradual process. You build up to a friendship. So don't start off acting chummy unless they initiate it—or they've reciprocated lesser things and seem receptive. Feel out the situation. Social butterflies may be unfazed by your good nature. But other people may view your friendliness with suspicion. "I don't know you like that," they may think, "What do you want from me?"

Second, the best conversations flow naturally. It's helpful to research the people you'll meet and bring up points of commonality. But don't overdo it. One or two details is enough; beyond that it can feel forced. Keep it to publicly available information. Most people don't appreciate a stranger knowing too much. There's a fine line between being flattered and creeped out. Feel free to mention where you saw the information too. Then ask questions and listen. Don't just regurgitate what you found.

Third, people are more than their demographics. Your similarities may suggest that you have common interests. But never assume. Just because you share a key trait—age, gender, race, religion—doesn't mean that you share core values. Our belief systems are informed by more than one dimension. Nor does it mean that they must favor you over those outside. I often hear this sentiment when a group is in the minority: "We need to band together." Be mindful that not everyone feels that way.

Fourth, relatability requires a level of vulnerability. People can't relate to a saint or a superhero. Let down your guard a bit. Admit that you don't have it all figured out. Share your doubts, past mistakes, and character flaws where appropriate. But be careful not to go overboard. Don't offload your personal problems on others. Use discretion. Some things are too much, too soon, taboo, or a fatal flaw. You're encouraged to be vulnerable up to a point. You can convey a message without getting explicit.

Finally, people have different boundaries. I integrate my personal and professional networks. Most successful leaders I know do as well. But some people prefer to keep their work separate from their home lives. They cut the chitchat short. Attempts at relating may feel invasive to them. When in doubt, go no further. Recognize that not everyone wants to be your friend—and that's perfectly fine. Don't push it. Don't take it personally. The nature of each relationship is determined by both parties.

Your good intentions will be reciprocated by some and rejected by others. It will be embraced by some and questioned by others. That doesn't mean you did anything wrong. Nor does it imply that they are bad people. What they want from you may just not align with what you offer. My friend Erik Alkire once reminded me of this truth. That person didn't appreciate your kind gesture, he said, but someone else would've loved it. As they say, go where you're celebrated, not tolerated. In the same way, exercise discernment, so you can approach each relationship in the manner most welcome.

CLOSING THOUGHTS

People want to work with those they know, like, and trust. When you are relatable, they will want you on their team. They will buy your products or support your projects. They will keep you in mind and choose you over your competitors. Opportunities will flow your way.

Being relatable makes you memorable. People will know you beyond mere awareness that you exist. They will view you not as a caricature or a collection of attributes but as a friend, a neighbor, a person worthy of respect. They will treat you in ways that makes you feel seen.

People will like you because they see a part of themselves in you. They feel like they understand you. And as importantly, they feel like you understand them as well. There's an assumed camaraderie, an inherent fellowship, a warmth that comes from being birds of a feather.

People will trust you to a greater extent than they otherwise might. If you're like them, the logic goes, then you hold similar values and priorities. You can be counted on to do the right things and act in proper ways. They will feel comfortable welcoming you into their network.

That said, warm fuzzy feelings aren't enough. People may know who you are but not what you can do. They may like you as a person but not as a professional. They may trust your character but not your competence. Let's settle these issues as we examine the final element: Credibility.

Element 5:
CREDIBILITY

Every week I meet startup founders who are tackling major problems. Many have ambitious visions, interesting ideas, and polished slide decks. But the most promising founders have one thing in common: They can attract people to themselves: Employees who buy into their vision. Investors who are willing to bet on them. Customers who pay before there's a finished product.

Why are people drawn to them? Usually, it's because they've built up some form of credibility. Through their traits, experience, reputation, or clarity of communication, they instill confidence in others. Their words feel reassuring. Their visions appear within reach. People trust them to deliver.

Now whether that trust is justified is a different story. One might say that credibility, like beauty, is in the eye of the beholder. What one person considers impressive, another may deem insufficient. What's admired in one community may go unappreciated in another. Indeed, people have different standards and priorities, biases and expectations.

But the point is that credibility is attractive. Credible businesses attract more customers. Credible nonprofits attract more donors. Credible employers attract higher-caliber employees. Likewise, credible individuals attract the attention of employers, investors, their peers, and the public.

People may not always know the value you bring. Based on their limited information, they may decline to meet with you. They may ignore your calls and emails. Most of us have experienced this rejection. Though it may be their loss, you likely miss out as well. This is where credibility comes in.

Credibility signals that you have value to offer. That you know your stuff. That you can get the job done. It gives people a reason to want to know you. It piques their interest to learn more about you. It makes them more willing to spend time with you.

This can play out in several ways: 1) Some people will have heard of you. Perhaps they attended your talk at a conference or read about your work online. So they contact you to get acquainted or to do business together; 2) Others will not have heard of you. But when you reach out to them, they will see who you are and respond, because they recognize your affiliations and respect your experiences; and 3) People who know you will introduce you to others. In this way, they can provide value to their networks. What will they say about you? They will highlight what makes you credible.

We've now come full circle. From the outset, we've established that value is the foundation for our relationships. In this chapter, we'll explore building credibility to open more relational doors.

The levers of credibility

We'll begin with a fundamental question: Where does credibility come from? Not which traits would make you appear credible—we'll get to those in a moment—but what levers can you pull to highlight what you have? Is credibility based on self-positioning, or is it conferred onto you by others?

The short answer is both. Building credibility is part personal branding, part social proof. There should be congruence between what you say and what others say about you. When aligned, these create a flywheel effect. How you position yourself leads to opportunities for social proof. And external validation can be incorporated into your personal brand. Instead of starting from square one in each context, you become known in ever-widening circles. Credibility sustains your networking momentum.

Let's take a closer look at personal branding and social proof.

Personal branding. Many people can discuss their work all day. They can speak about their industry without preparation. But ask them to describe themselves or write a personal statement, and they freeze up. They stumble through their words. They aren't used to talking about themselves.

Yet to be credible, you must be known. And to be known, you must put yourself out there. Not in shameless self-promotion, but in confident self-representation. You must be your own advocate. If you won't do it, nobody else will do it for you. Nobody else can or should do it for you.

This applies to both employees and entrepreneurs. I often meet first-time founders who say they will hire a marketer to promote the brand or a sales executive to pitch to investors. No, I correct them, that is *your* job—at least in the early days. As the founder, it is *your* story to tell.

So get over the nervous tension. Push through your doubts and insecurities. If you want to be seen as an industry expert or a community leader, you must position yourself that way. The more often you do it, the more natural it becomes. And as we've established, when you feel comfortable in your own skin, you'd be viewed as more authentic, confident, trustworthy—indeed, more credible.

The goal here is not to launch a marketing campaign. By personal branding, I'm not talking about logos, fonts, or colors. Though some people may choose to differentiate themselves with visual assets, those aren't necessary for everyone. Here I simply mean presenting yourself in a genuine and favorable way. Be clear on what you're about and intentional in conveying that image.

We had discussed telling people what you're doing. Either they will help, or they will get out of your way. Let's take that idea a step further: Tell people what you want them to know about you. Frame it for them in a meaningful, memorable way. Why? Because if you don't create a narrative for yourself, others will come up with their own interpretations—which are often less generous than you'd like.

You want to get ahead of any negative perceptions. You want to tell your side of the story. The good news is that you can. People want to quickly make sense of information. They don't trust what they don't understand. And most won't spend the time to figure you out. So just give it to them. Usually, they will latch onto what you say about yourself, assuming you can reasonably back up your claims.

This is personal branding at its core. Identify two or three things you want people to remember about you. These should be more like themes than bullet points. Distill them into a compelling narrative. Connect the dots for others. Who are you, and why should they care? Then live it out every day. Practice what you preach. Demonstrate it by your words and actions, both in public and in private.

Social proof. What you say about yourself is not enough. Anyone can brag. But how reliable are your claims? How accurate are your stories? How balanced is your self-assessment? Even if you speak the truth, people may be skeptical unless you have corroborating evidence.

You might call yourself a team player, but would your coworkers agree? You might claim to deliver results, but would your manager attest to that? You might boast about your empathy or your character, but would your closest friends concur? What do other people say about you? What do they say when you're not around? What are they willing to say on the record and without reservation?

Perhaps social proof is best illustrated in business: "logos of brands you've worked with, testimonials from previous clients, reviews of your product, or confirmation that others have purchased your service."[1] By associating with you, a third party confers some of their credibility onto you. Social proof acts as a shorthand for the value you offer. It signals to others that you are worth engaging with.

The more known and credible you are, the more people will pay attention to you—which, in turn, will spark curiosity in those beyond your immediate reach. Your reputation will precede you.

See, credibility is inherently social. Whenever there's incomplete information, people look to others for cues on what to do. If all their friends are buying a certain product, watching a certain movie, or using a certain app, they may check it out as well. They want to be in the know. They want to make their own judgment call. Likewise, if you're seen as credible, as someone to know, others will approach you to see for themselves. In this way, credibility compounds the value of your network.

If you're outstanding in your field, you may even take on a pseudo-celebrity status. People will want to rub shoulders with you, not because of what you can do for them but just to say that they know you. They gain a story to tell and clout among their peers. "We worked in the same department!" or "I once met him in an elevator!" they excitedly proclaim. You may not be a movie star or a professional athlete, and your fan club may be quite small, but the point stands: Remarkable people draw attention.

Now social proof may take the form of references and testimonials. That is, somebody vouches for you or advocates on your behalf. But more often, what we call social proof comes from proxies—passive markers of credibility. Let me explain and show you how to use these for your benefit.

Perceptions and proxies

We must make a distinction between perceived versus demonstrated credibility.

Throughout life, we're judged on fairly crude measures. Think of college applications. We're evaluated on our high school GPAs, test scores, and extracurriculars. In theory, past behavior predicts future behavior. The straight-A student should continue to excel. Therefore, he should be admitted.

In practice, these are weak predictors of college performance. GPAs are affected by countless factors. SAT scores reflect test-taking skills more than intellect. Extracurriculars tend to bias against those with lesser means. These variables may be proxies for responsibility and grit. But admissions decisions are more subjective than people realize. Colleges make do with the data points they can get.

Likewise, most people don't know very much about you. They haven't seen your work. So they use mental shortcuts or proxy measures to size you up. They form an opinion based on publicly available information: your titles and employers, your degrees and alma maters, the sections you filled out on LinkedIn, or the highlights you included in a personal bio. These things guide how they perceive you.

Perception may not be reality, but it can certainly affect the outcome. So don't ignore these proxies and stamps of approval. Just remember that they themselves are not the end goal. Here are a few common ones.

Degrees and credentials. Like it or not, people make assumptions based on what you studied and where you went to school. Their expectations may be informed by the college's reputation or their experience with its alumni. They may also hold certain majors in higher regard than others.

Now your job isn't to defend your school or major. It's to represent yourself. Don't flaunt your degree; nobody likes a braggart. But don't sell yourself short either. Leverage what you have.

I used to downplay my bachelor's degree in social psychology. To me, it wasn't as impressive as business or engineering or the hard sciences. It wasn't nearly as in demand. I felt like my undergrad education could be summed up: "Is this due to nature or nurture? Why not both!" Whenever someone asked me what I had studied, I mumbled the answer and moved onto the next topic.

One day a hospital executive named Johan Otter set me straight. He had great respect for psychology as a field. Regardless of what the college curriculum did or didn't cover, he told me, there's no reason to be shy about my degree. There's no gain in speaking poorly of it. Likewise, own what you have. You earned it. You can't control others' perceptions, but there's no need to dismiss yourself.

Employer brands. People also form impressions based on where you work or have worked. If they're an industry insider, this perception may mean something. But most people are not. Either they've heard of your company and hold an opinion on it, or they haven't. So it's biased toward large employers over smaller ones, consumer businesses over B2B operations. That makes this proxy rather irrational. Yet it's ubiquitous. So let's discuss how your employer brand affects your networking.

It's easy when you work for a well-known employer. Fortune 500 corporations. Big Three consulting firms. FAANG tech companies. People are drawn to household names. The credibility of the brand rubs off on you. People assume that you must be capable if you work there. They believe that you, as an individual or through your employer, can offer them value. So they're willing and eager to speak with you. They will invite you into rooms that were formerly closed off. Use this to your advantage. A respected employer brand paves the way.

The downside is that many people will contact you solely for their own gain. They have little interest in you as a person. They only want what you can do for them. Strangers will ask you for job referrals. Vendors will pitch you irrelevant products. Random people will want to "pick your brain." If you don't set firm boundaries and guard your time, you'll become overwhelmed by these junk requests.

If you work for a lesser-known employer—a small business, local nonprofit, or early-stage startup—that brand carries less weight. Most people haven't heard of the company, so it means little to them that you work there. Without switching jobs, how can you make the most of the employer brand for networking? It's a matter of putting yourself in the right places and emphasizing the right details.

First, the general public may not care about the company, but professionals in your niche may be impressed. I was an early employee at a SaaS startup called PrescribeWellness. To most people, that name doesn't ring a bell. But to many in the independent pharmacy space, it holds significance. We had released some excellent products and were acquired for $150 million. Every so often, I meet a pharmacy owner or healthtech founder who's excited to talk because I had worked there.

Second, people in adjacent verticals may be curious. In my early 20s, I attended many healthcare networking events. The majority of people I met worked for hospitals and health systems. They were intrigued by my startup job because it was novel to them. I had a story to tell. I knew things that they didn't. So I stood out from my peers. Had I worked at a local hospital, they would've viewed me as just another new grad. Sometimes their unfamiliarity with the brand works in your favor.

Third, they may not have heard of your employer, but they may recognize its clients and partners. Perhaps your biotech startup is collaborating with the Mayo Clinic. Or your nutrition products are on the shelves at Whole Foods. Or your IT services firm has been a long-time contractor for NASA. Small businesses gain credibility from working with larger brands. You can do the same.

Other affiliations. Outside of work, what professional and civic activities are you involved in? Do you serve on an advisory board? Do you volunteer with a nonprofit? Do you speak at industry events? Do you mentor students at the local college? Some brand affiliations would ring a bell with the average person. But most carry weight only within a niche group. So aim to be relevant, rather than to impress.

Choose quality over quantity. Don't rattle off everything you've ever done. Highlight key affiliations that lend credibility. What do they add qualitatively? For example, your first adjunct lecturer role shows that you teach. Listing a second or third appointment makes little difference. I've taught at three colleges now. The first one gave me experience for which I'm grateful, but it wasn't a respected institution. I've since taught at more reputable schools, so I no longer include it on my resume.

Affiliations add depth and color to your professional image. In one sense, they're akin to extracurriculars for college applicants. Many students have strong GPAs and test scores. But some play on the basketball team or in the marching band; others serve in student government or at the children's hospital. They stand out from their peers. They are more memorable to admissions officers. Likewise, your involvements set you apart. They indicate that there's more to you than your job title.

This becomes especially relevant should you want to make a career pivot. See, it's easy to get pigeonholed, to be known for one thing only. I've met people at all levels who wrestle with this. One executive wanted to be known for strategy, but colleagues just viewed him as the data guy. Similarly, you may aspire to rebrand yourself. Perhaps you want to move to a different industry. Or you want to switch functions within the same field. Outside affiliations help to redefine your image. They show that you are exposed to the right people and experiences. They make you more agile in your career.

One caveat: Represent your affiliations accurately. Don't stretch the truth. Don't exaggerate your involvement or influence in the organization. If you mislead people, it will come back to haunt you.

Awards and honors. The value of an award is not to stroke your ego. It's not to replay what you've already accomplished. It's to get you noticed for new opportunities. Don't focus on the award itself; think about how to use it. My friend Aaron Byzak says that employers like to hire award-winning staff. He's an executive with four Emmy Awards to his name. These things mean something to somebody.

Now there are countless awards out there. Every company, magazine, and blogger seem to dole them out these days. As I see it, an award is only as legitimate as its source. People in the know can sniff out rubbish in an instant. Admittedly, the public may be swayed by pay-for-play schemes. But those are not the kind you want. To add credibility, pursue reputable awards and accolades.

Many people see their peers winning an award, receiving an honor, or being featured in some list—and they wonder, "Why don't I ever get chosen?" Well, did you apply for it? Here's something they don't tell you: If you want that award, you need to apply or have a friend nominate you. Or you must know the right people and be visible to them. Most awards are not based on pure merit.

Yes, there are cases where you may be found. If you're prominent in your field, more opportunities will come your way. Just like there are times a recruiter may reach out to you about a role. But most people, in most cases, had applied for their jobs. The same is true for awards and honors.

You may be "chosen" for an award. You may be "recognized" for your achievements. You may be "selected," presumably through some rigorous process. Such rhetoric carries an air of importance. The truth is: People are indeed "chosen" but usually from a pool of candidates, not from the universe at large. Awards don't fall out of the sky. More often than not, you must make the first move.

Follower count. As we had discussed, people take cues from others on where to direct their attention. This remains true even when those others are strangers. Even when they're just aggregate statistics. Think of bestselling books, blockbuster movies, or Billboard-charting songs. These all boast how many people they've reached, how many units they've sold, how much attention they've garnered.

All things being equal, credibility favors the larger number. Restaurants with more Yelp reviews. Amazon products with more verified purchases. Newsletters with more subscribers. People gravitate toward that which is popular. So numbers showing scale do matter. To be clear, it's not about the absolute number but the presumed safety of being in good company: "All those people can't be wrong." Yet even when they are, one may feel less regret for having followed the crowd.

Does having the most followers make you the leading expert? No. But it does signify that people want to hear from you. There's quantifiable value in this distribution, especially when it's concentrated among a profession or demographic. Advertisers want to reach engaged audiences. Conference organizers want speakers who draw a large crowd. Record labels want artists, and book publishers want authors, who bring ready customers. All that said, quality is important. Having 100 raving fans is better than 1,000 lukewarm contacts or 10,000 bots, fake followers, and dormant accounts.

Appearance. Credibility is not all about standing out. Sometimes the goal is to fit in. As a grad student, I attended an event at a mentor's hospital. I thought it went well. Afterward, he asked whether I noticed how others had dressed. Yes, much more formally than I had. He told me: "Don't let people discount you based on your appearance. If you want to be taken seriously, you must look the part."[2]

Dress codes vary across professions and industries. Bankers and hospital executives dress more formally than artists and tech founders. A suit and tie may look out of place at a creative studio, just as shorts and a t-shirt are inappropriate in the boardroom. You want to dress for the occasion—and as fashion experts advise, just one step above those around you.

Now some people object that their appearance has no bearing on the quality of their work. Though that may be true, it's wise to observe the context. Even Steve Jobs, known for his black turtlenecks, wore formal suits when meeting with creditors.

The company you keep. When you are seen with intelligent people, you're assumed to be smart. When you are seen with wealthy people, you're assumed to be rich. When you are seen with famous people, you're assumed to be someone to know. Most people associate with others like themselves.

We also influence these perceptions by how we communicate. David Anderson, former GM at Amazon, shares this example: Let's say you meet someone who tells you that they manage people at Google. That's great, but you have no clue how senior they are. They could be a frontline manager or a vice president. Then they mention a recent chat with a VP. In his words: "Wham. You're now convinced that they're a senior employee. Certainly, not entry level. They are likely Director or VP level. How does that work? Because you tend to interact with people around your level of seniority."[3]

This is not a license to name-drop. Nor should you befriend people just for the halo effect. But recognize that others do form impressions based on who's around you and how you talk about them.

Keep in mind that proxy measures are mere estimations of credibility. Outside the top schools, for example, most are a mixed bag. The brightest students at state colleges often rival those at elite universities. I've had friends who were accepted to Ivy Leagues but—for personal or financial reasons—chose a less prestigious school. Plus, even top universities may be weak in certain disciplines.

Because of these limitations, don't dismiss yourself if you lack the desired traits. Don't get cocky if you have them. Proxies can be summed up by the saying: "All models are wrong, but some are useful."

Credibility demonstrated

External markers are fine, but there must be substance behind the show, proof behind the promise. Depth, nuance, and specificity—these separate the expert from the charlatan. You may look the part. But what can you do? How do you back up your claims to credibility? Consider the following.

Past experience. Here we're not talking about "years of experience" but actual know-how. Employers and customers want assurance that you can solve their problems. The strongest evidence is having done the work before—preferably for a company of similar size and scope. Can you speak about it in depth? What was the situation? What did you do and why? And what were the outcomes?

Conference hosts want to see that you understand their audiences. That you've walked in their shoes. That you speak with authority, not as an armchair critic or ivory tower researcher. For instance, you don't just theorize about managing a remote workforce. You've done it and can speak to the challenges. You don't just speculate about what a failing company should do. You've led a turnaround and can share actual stories. You've been in the trenches, and you wear your battle scars with pride.

Here's another way to view it: Experience means that you can tell what's normal and what's not. You understand how the process is supposed to go. You know how things should look along the way.

Take any process. Most people can tell you the current state. That's a matter of observation. They may visualize the finished product or ideal state as well. But in between, things get murkier for a novice. The intermediate steps may not be intuitive. They may not resemble the final product at all.

Let's say you're baking a cake for the first time. (If you're a decent baker, substitute cake with something more complex like macarons or a soufflé.) You know how the result should look and taste. You have all the ingredients and step-by-step instructions. But at certain points, you may ask yourself: Is it supposed to look like this? Did I get the consistency right? Why is it doing that?

But after several times, you've become familiar with the process. You know what to look for. You can spot and avoid newbie mistakes. You can distinguish acceptable errors from causes for concern.

That's the value of experience. Whether you develop software or fix machinery or negotiate contracts, having done it many times, you can keep the process on track. You can spot red flags and call out nonsense when necessary. You can get the job done right the first time. That's why you are credible.

Public activities. Most people haven't worked with you. They haven't seen you in action. You may be skilled, but they'd have to take your word for it—unless you show them. For some professions, that means pointing to your portfolio. For others, it means writing, speaking, and being visible with your ideas. Share your thoughts publicly. This is a low-risk way to give others a sense of who you are.

For many people, speaking is a natural step in building credibility. When you speak at an event, or on a podcast or a webinar, you showcase your expertise to potential employers, customers, and peers. You are seen as an industry leader. You get immediate recognition from this audience. Moreover, afterward you can say that you had presented there. Think of the relatively unknown people who spoke at a local TEDx event. That carries some weight and distinguishes them from competitors later on.

What should you speak about? Choose topics that matter to your audience, that fit the spirit of the occasion, and on which you have some authority. Play to your strengths. Know your material inside and out. You should be able to give both a succinct overview and a detailed explanation. Most of all, speak on topics you care about. The most compelling talks come from the heart, from lived experience, from a personal connection to the topic. Embody your subject and speak with conviction.

Depending on your topic, you may speak at colleges or professional associations, churches or chambers of commerce. Go where your target audience is. There you will provide the most value and find the most relevant relationships. In many cases, you will need to reach out and introduce yourself. Tell them what you speak about and why it matters for their members. Some groups may fit you into their programming. Others may host a dedicated event for your topic. They may give you 10 minutes or an hour. Don't be picky early on. Take the opportunities as they come. Over time people will recognize who you are. They may have heard you speak elsewhere and invite you to come present to their group.

Consider your motivations for speaking. Be aware that many organizations will not have a budget to pay you for it. My lens here is on networking and building your brand as an industry expert—not a full-time professional speaker. So the speaking is not about making money. It's about developing relationships and credibility. It's about a broader vision on a longer time table.

Now this is important: Respect your audience. This applies whether you're speaking to a large crowd or a small group, to business executives or college students. Though their eyes are on you, the event is not about you—it's about them. So come prepared. Connect your message to their needs. Answer their burning questions. Offer real value to them. Don't sell from the stage or read from a script. Don't flaunt your greatness or go off on tangents. Focus on your audience and their interests. Seek to educate, inspire, motivate, and entertain. A successful talk is one that the audience finds worthwhile.

Writing is another way to build credibility. It gives people a glimpse into what you know and how you think. So don't just parrot what others are saying. Go beyond regurgitating facts and figures, platitudes and clichés. Formulate a thesis, take a stance, own your position. You can also document your journey as you build in public. Share your triumphs, trials, and takeaways. You don't need to be the foremost expert on a subject. But you must have an angle, a differentiator—a fresh way of looking at things, a more digestible format, or something unique to your personal style and delivery.

Speaking of style, I once read a quote in a how-to book that was surprisingly profound: "Style is like a person, with all their shortcomings, flashes of brilliance, and vulnerability. A guarded, poised, elegant style may be admired in the way a person with those qualities might, but it will rarely be loved."[4] The world needs your views in your voice—not a piece of corporate propaganda with all the personality wrung out of it. The level of formality is your call. But don't worry about sounding like an expert with flawless grammar and highfalutin jargon. True experts need not parade their scholarship.

Authenticity is key. A blog I write for offers this guidance: "It's important to strike a balance of having some authority or clear opinion on a subject without acting like we have all the answers."[5] I believe this captures the essence of credibility for networking. Readers want the real you, warts and all.

Don't forget about distribution. Where do you plan to publish? If you write your own blog or newsletter, you will have full editorial control. You can say whatever you want however you want. The catch is that you need to build an audience. Otherwise, you'd spend hours writing with no one to read it.

Or you can write for an established publication. You gain credibility for being published in it, and your articles will find an existing readership. However, your content is subject to approval, and your schedule may not match their editorial calendar. If you take this route, be sure to read the publication. Familiarize yourself with their audience and house style. Consider whether it's a fit for your brand.

Press coverage. Next, let's talk about earned media and publicity. Perhaps you're not a writer yourself, but you have experiences and insights that reporters seek. You can share these as a source for their stories. Getting quoted in a prominent paper or trade journal brings instant credibility. It holds more weight than what you write on your own blog. That's because a respected third-party deemed your views worthy of inclusion. Plus, it's neat to see your name in the newspaper. Let me give you a crash course on media relations.

First, understand the role of journalists. They are not your marketing team. They do not serve you. Their job is not to make you look good. They serve their editors and audiences. Their job is to tell engaging stories and accurately represent the facts. They know the articles they want to write, and if you fit the profile, they may interview you. But you have no control over the content or the angle. That's not a negative; it's how journalism works. Recognize that, so there will be no misunderstandings. As a PR firm might tell its clients: If you want to control the narrative, there are things called advertisements.

Second, pitch to the right reporters. Look for those covering your industry or subject. Read their recent articles. Know who they are and what they write about. Few things irk journalists more than receiving pitches outside their beat. A healthcare reporter has no use for entertainment news. A sports reporter doesn't care about manufacturing trends. Spraying and praying doesn't work. This may sound obvious, but it happens every day. Irrelevant pitches show that you don't respect their time or intellect.

Third, make it easy for them to work with you. Journalists are busy people. They have deadlines upon deadlines. For some stories, the reporter may want to speak with you. For others, they just need written comment. Be responsive and accommodating. You may also want to cultivate a relationship over time. Engage with them before pitching anything. Speak on background about industry issues. Share thoughtful analyses and predictions. When they get a relevant assignment, guess whom they will call?

Finally, give reporters what they need. Provide usable quotes, organized bullet points, and clear perspectives. Capture their attention with real substance. Stand out by using what I call the four Ps.

- Prompt: Make your pitches timely and relevant. Why does this matter now? If there's a query, respond as soon as possible. A few hours later may be too late. Prompt has a second meaning, as in "answering the prompt." In your eagerness, don't forget to answer the question.

- Personal: Reporters need concrete examples and first-person accounts. Not what could happen, but what did happen. Not what you heard through the grapevine, but what you witnessed and experienced. Stories of individuals bring the trends, statistics, and broader narratives to life.
- Practical: People read articles for more than enjoyment. In many cases, they look for ideas to improve their lives, careers, and businesses. If you're asked for expert comment, include actionable advice. If you're relating a personal account, share tips and lessons learned.
- Provocative: No, I don't mean racy or offensive. But your content should provoke thought. Most people out there say similar things. Conformity is not newsworthy. Challenge conventional wisdom and commonly held beliefs. People pay attention to that which is unexpected.

All that said, publicity tends to be fleeting. As I see it, press is a cherry-on-top achievement. Saying you've been quoted in *The New York Times* or *The Wall Street Journal* sounds impressive. It goes well at the end of a personal bio. But in its absence, not much is missed. So don't spend too much time chasing the press. It's only one brushstroke on your canvas of credibility.

Personal excellence. In the opening vignette, I talked about scouting for early-stage startups. One powerful signal is when a company has the backing of a top-tier venture firm. Suddenly, other investors will also want in. Why? Because the startup gained a "bridge loan of credibility in advance of tangible evidence."[6] Key words: in advance of. The tangible evidence will sooner or later be due.

Likewise, people are drawn to your markers of credibility. They believe you are credible due to your reputation—or that of your school or employer. That's how it starts. But reputation only takes you so far. Once people have met you, they will judge you based on what they observe and experience for themselves. And that conclusion will override anything that may have come prior.

I may hear that someone has a strong work ethic. If it came from a trusted source, I'd believe it and expect accordingly. I'd know it by reputation. But once I've worked with that person, I will have seen them in action and know for myself. I will be able to vouch for them. "Based on my experience, John is hardworking and reliable" holds more weight than "I heard that John is a hard worker."

On the flip side, if John doesn't live up to his reputation, I'd soon find out as well. Initially, there may be some grace due to the "bridge loan of credibility." Perhaps he was having an off day. Life happens. But if John continued failing to pull his weight, he'd deplete any borrowed credibility he had left.

You don't want to be that guy or gal. That hurts not only your reputation but your relationships too. It reflects poorly on the people who had invested in, vouched for, or introduced you. You let them down or made them look bad. So they may not help you again. Your reputation shouldn't mislead people, just as your resume shouldn't exaggerate. Whatever you present is subject to scrutiny, so seek excellence in everything you do.

Embracing who you are

All this talk of credibility may trigger in you what has been called imposter syndrome. You may feel like you don't deserve to be where you are. You may downplay your assets or traits. You feel uncomfortable owning your credibility. Allow me to offer some perspective.

First, imposter syndrome is not mere lack of confidence. Nor does it mean general anxiety and nervousness. Like many popular terms, it gets co-opted, and the meaning becomes watered down.

Let's be clear: You can only have imposter syndrome if you are capable at what you do. You have the requisite skills and abilities to perform your job. By objective measures, you meet or exceed expectations. Yet you discount yourself and feel like you don't belong. *That* is imposter syndrome.

If someone is not capable at their job, and they feel anxious about it, that is not imposter syndrome. They can't discount themselves because they don't bring value to discount from. In many cases, the more suitable term is the Peter principle: People get promoted to their level of incompetence.

The further you advance in your career, the more you will encounter peers and managers who have no business being in the roles they occupy. They may have been strong individual contributors. They may have attended the top schools or worked at blue chip companies. But they aren't effective at their jobs today.

Likewise, you will see people who appear to be ubiquitous. Every industry has these so-called thought leaders. They speak at all the conferences. They are on podcasts and in trade publications. They have large online followings. Seeing their popularity may raise your own insecurities.

But "no one is as popular as they seem," explains David Burkus. They merely "create the illusion of majority" by knowing the right people and being in the right places at the right time. One can have "the appearance of being everywhere and in demand—by only focusing on a few of the right connections."[7]

The cruel irony of imposter syndrome is that many high-performers doubt themselves in the presence of those less qualified—

colleagues who make up in confidence and charisma what they lack in skill.

This is even more pronounced among minorities in a given context—the only woman in the room, the only Asian American in leadership, and so on. Traits unrelated to the work itself. They may misattribute the source of their anxiety. "I feel out of place because I am unworthy," they tell themselves, yet the more accurate framing may be, "I feel out of place because I am different."

Imposter syndrome also rears its ugly head following a career change or a promotion. Transitions, even positive ones, may usher in feelings of doubt and self-consciousness. In your prior role, perhaps you were a leader or an expert. You knew the ins and outs of your job. You've done it for years. People looked up to you. They even benchmarked their performance against the standards you have set.

But now you're the newbie, asking basic questions and making rookie mistakes. It's humbling. You feel small and insecure. You don't want to let others down. Though you hold the title, you aren't sure that you have what it takes. Job and career transitions can often feel destabilizing.

One individual couldn't understand why he felt so anxious, even after accepting the role he wanted. I shared with him this perspective: You're leaving a known situation for an unknown one. In your old job, you were familiar with your workload, what your boss expected of you, what success looked like. You had certain rhythms and processes and ways of doing your work.

You knew the people, the culture, the leadership styles. You understood which behaviors were rewarded and which were not. Perhaps you had been there a while and saw how the company had evolved. Not only did you know all these things, you yourself were a known entity. People recognized who you were and what you did. You had built rapport with and earned respect from those around you.

In your new job, you're starting from scratch. Though you expect it to be positive, there are many uncertainties. So it's natural to feel nervous. But your anxiety doesn't speak to your ability. Your lack of confidence doesn't reflect your level of competence. Don't worry. You'll find your groove soon enough. Remember: They had chosen you over all the other applicants. There is a reason for that.

Change can be nerve-racking even in your own organization. I once confided in a mentor that I felt a lot of pressure following a promotion. I wanted to prove that I deserved it. His response: "I recommend that you keep a perspective on 'pressure.' Are you doing anything that thousands of people haven't done before? Probably not. Are you going to succeed or fail significantly more than others before you? Probably not. Ultimately, things are never as big a deal as we make them out to be."

I found those words sobering. There's comfort in seeing the bigger picture. It makes you feel small but not in the same way that insecurity does. It reminds you that you are not alone. You are not an imposter. Up close, the obstacles may look daunting. The learning curves may appear insurmountable. But take a step back, zoom out, shift your focus, and things inevitably fall into their rightful places.

Self-awareness is key to combating your imposter syndrome. You must be your own advocate, even as you wrestle with crushing doubt. In those moments, pause and question your assumptions. Fight the feelings with facts. Recenter yourself with concrete examples of your performance. You've done it once, and you can do it again. You've endured harder trials and overcome tougher challenges. You are capable, you are credible, and you are worth knowing. Whatever life holds, bring it on.

CLOSING THOUGHTS

My dad once told me a Vietnamese saying that roughly translates: "Those nearby are impressed by your character; those afar are impressed by your appearance." Literally, your clothes. People at a distance look upon the external. They're attracted to your credentials and reputation—the appearance of credibility. But to those who know you, what truly matters is your character and the quality of your work.

If you claim to be an expert, back it up with evidence. If you say you support a cause, demonstrate it through your actions. If you boast of your sound judgment, your outcomes should reflect that. If you present yourself as reliable, your friends and neighbors should agree.

In fact, who you are becomes amplified up close. Acquaintances may say that you're nice, but friends know the depth of your kindness. Outsiders may assume that you're smart, but teammates can attest to your mental caliber. Relationships demand substance, not mere optics. Up close, it's hard to fake it. It's difficult to hide. If your public image is incongruent with who you are in private, that discrepancy will be amplified as well—and disappointment can be far worse than disregard.

Credibility must be grounded in truth, or else it won't last. Without a solid foundation, the cracks will start to show. Sooner or later the façade will crumble. But if you're a person of substance who seeks the good of others, your credibility will be acknowledged, and your network will multiply.

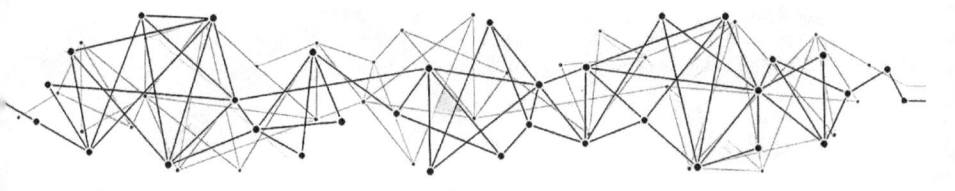

CONCLUSION

In college, I began a habit of talking with random people, not because I was an extrovert but precisely because I wasn't. I'd strike up conversations while standing in line, waiting in lobbies, or sitting in cafes. A brief exchange beat glancing at each other awkwardly. Nine out of 10 times, I found myself glad to have had the conversation. Some of those encounters led to lasting friendships.

I realized there were people I had seen around—classmates and neighbors whom I had passed by many times—yet we had never spoken a word to one another. I made a point to say hi to them.

Likewise, I'd engage in conversation with the supermarket cashier, the bank teller, the employee making my burrito at Chipotle. Those minute or two felt less transactional and more human.

Without interaction we're prone to assume. People may appear cold, standoffish, even hostile. They may have a hard look to them; their faces say stay away. Or they just seem so different that there's no apparent reason for you to talk. But a quick chat reveals how friendly they are or how much you have in common. And guess what? They may have had the same assumptions about you.

Moreover, people today are lonely. They crave social connection. In our modern world, it's easy to feel invisible—like you're just a face in the crowd. Research suggests that everyday conversations "build the sense of community and belonging to a larger social structure."[1] In layman's terms, we can all make the world feel warmer, safer, and more connected. Often it begins with a simple hello.

My early experiences sowed the seeds for the framework in this book. To recap, the five elements of professional networking are value, initiative, consistency, relatability, and credibility. The first three lay the foundation for all our relationships. The latter two take things up a notch.

These are to be applied in conjunction, not in silos. You don't graduate from the foundational elements. For example, don't try to build credibility without offering value to others. It's self-centered and short-sighted. Your relationships will be shallow, transactional, and fleeting. Likewise, don't expect your warmth and relatability to make up for lack of initiative. That's reactive and restrictive. You will miss out on valuable connections and opportunities. And without consistency, there can be no progress, no momentum, no deepening of relationships. All five elements must be put into practice.

Now I'd like to share a few parting thoughts. Consider these as the exhortation of a friend who cares—not only for your career or business success but about you as an individual.

Being a good, solid person

To build healthy relationships, you must be a genuine, considerate person. Give people reason to like and trust you. That requires integrity in your words and actions. It calls for empathy in your attitude and approach. It demands excellence in your personal and professional standards.

These things don't come from sheer willpower. They begin with a renewed frame of mind. Lift your perspective to see the people, the need, the beauty, the wonder around you. Donald Miller is a gifted storyteller who has helped millions tell their own stories. He shares: "The most difficult lie I have ever contended with is this: Life is a story about me."[2] Indeed, it's not all about you either.

I can't teach you to be virtuous. But it helps to remember the Golden Rule: Do unto others as you would have them do unto you. Perhaps not literally, as our preferences vary. But maintain the spirit of loving your neighbor as yourself. Treat them with the respect and goodness that you would like to be shown. You know when you're not being completely honest. You know when you're feeling a qualm about your actions. You know when you're using someone or asking too much for the relationship.

"Nothing is free," says Anneliese Pixton, an educator and edtech founder. "Someone gives it to you at a loss to themselves, or you give up something in return. The exchange might be money, data, time, or expertise. But nothing is free." Relationships are about give and take. If you reach out to people and seldom get a response, check the equation.[3] There's a clear line between being bold and acting entitled. Before hitting send, consider whether you'd respond favorably to a message like this.

It all comes back to self-awareness. Some people take too much or talk too much. Meanwhile, others are afraid to ask, to speak up, to take up space. Personal improvement will look different for each group. The former should tone it down, listen more, and seek first the good of others. The latter need to recognize the value they offer and advocate more for themselves. Whichever camp you identify with, ask yourself: Am I acting in good faith? Am I considering it from the other person's point of view?

In addition, ask others for their perspectives of you. How you see yourself, your words and your actions, may differ from how other people view you. Now this takes courage and vulnerability. You may hear things you won't like. But don't get defensive. Be open to honest feedback, even if it may sting. Otherwise, people won't speak their minds, and you won't know what you should improve.

Pay attention to patterns. If one person says you're a jerk, that might reflect a bad interaction but not represent who you are. If 10 people say you're a jerk, there's probably some truth to it. Ask for specific examples. Apologize for grievances they may have against you. Express your willingness to learn and change. Commit to reducing those awkward, annoying, or abrasive things you do.

It's never too late to change. I once read in someone's bio: "I have said things I no longer agree with." This simple statement is full of wisdom. We'd all do well to demonstrate such humility and maturity. No need to deny or justify what you once believed or expressed. No need to beat yourself up or hide away in shame. If you realize that you had been wrong, admit it, whether the change is a 180-degree turn or a slight course correction. Then figure out how to act in light of your new beliefs. This is a helpful reminder for all of us. I suspect that we have all said or done things that we no longer agree with.

On a more positive note, listen to what people admire about you. Look for patterns there as well. Double down on what you're doing right. You may be appreciated in more ways than you realize.

Choosing the right friendships

Relationships don't just happen to us. We choose the people with whom we associate. We choose how much to let them into our lives. While interactions may be a function of circumstance, our friendships are a matter of choice. On this subject, there are three difficult realities you must accept.

First, not everyone is your friend. Not everyone should be your friend. Some people are toxic. They abuse your kindness, waste your time, and drain your energy. Instead of bringing joy, they sap it away. Instead of adding value, they destroy what exists. They are liars and thieves, bullies and manipulators. They care about nothing but profit, no one but themselves.

Avoid these people like the plague. Don't associate with them for a minute. They will bring stress to your life and harm to your reputation. As you build your network, you must also guard it from the leeches and troublemakers. Do not let in these bad actors. I cannot emphasize this enough.

Just as you hold yourself to core principles, you must also have standards for those you call friends. The closer they are to your inner circle, the higher your basic expectations should be.

If we think of the five elements as virtues to exhibit, the wrong companions not only lack them but embody their antitheses. They extract value that doesn't belong to them. They are lazy opportunists lying in wait. Their word is unreliable, their deeds inconsistent. They are out of touch and unempathetic to others. Their credentials are negative signals. They are not the type you want in your life.

Ultimately, people are the number one driver of your life satisfaction. The right friends will lift you up to new potentials. The wrong friends will drag you down to their level—and then step on you to climb up. Choose wisely. Surround yourself with good people.

Second, the right friends are not always apparent. You may overlook people based on their career, color, or creed. You may assume that you have little reason to associate. You may miss potential friendships when you are too focused elsewhere or preoccupied with the wrong crowd.

Most of all, you will miss good people if you are too guarded. You will stand alone if you close yourself off. I hope the preceding warning doesn't make you cynical. Yes, there are selfish people who bring nothing but trouble. But there are also good souls and kindred spirits who inspire life-giving joy.

To be clear, nobody is perfect. There's not a clean dichotomy between good and evil, saints and sinners. We all have the capacity for both virtues and vices. We act in our own self-interests. We have different goals, values, priorities, risk profiles, and communication styles. At times we will clash with one another. There will be arguments and misunderstandings. Good people can disagree on important issues.

But be careful not to become hardened by cynicism. In *Cardcaptor Sakura: Clear Card*, there's a scene where the title character is walking home with her friend Meiling Li. They are having a heart-to-heart in the warm glow of the sunset. Meiling tells Sakura that by seeing the good in people, she attracts good people into her life. Then she delivers the most poignant line I've ever heard in an anime: "And when you believe all the people around you are bad, you don't notice when you meet good people."[4] Pretty deep for an anime-only character—if you know, you know.

Third, relationships do not last forever. In most cases, there is no tension or hostility, no dramatic breakup or falling-out. People just drift apart. Friends move away, coworkers change jobs, classmates graduate and go on with their lives. There are fewer natural interactions, fewer shared contexts and purposes, fewer reasons to keep in touch. It takes more effort to maintain contact, effort that may not be fully embraced or reciprocated. So the relationship fizzles.

Perhaps an old friend or neighbor comes to mind, someone you wish you had kept in touch with. In some cases, you can reconnect and even deepen a friendship. Earlier in the book, I told you about two of my closest friends. I knew Dennis since elementary school, but we didn't become best friends until college. I met Gina my first week in grad school, but we didn't grow close until years later. So it's certainly possible for dormant friendships to blossom. But I'd say that's rare. These two were the exceptions, rather than the norm. For every relationship I've rekindled, dozens have faded away.

And that's okay. People are in your life for a season. They change over time, and so do you. As your interests and priorities diverge from one another's, the emotional distance between you increases. The conversations grow wearisome. The relationship becomes one-sided. Where there was chemistry, now there's only friction. Letting go of a friendship is difficult. It feels bittersweet. But sometimes that's the best you can do. Recollect the good times. Remember what you've learned. Accept it and move on.

Living with intentionality

When you are crystal clear about who you are and who your friends are—how you carry yourself and how you relate to the world—you can act more purposefully. You can stand more confidently. You can pursue goals more deliberately. You can live more intentionally.

Throughout life, there are things we do because we want to. And there are things we do because we feel like we "have to"—or we've been told that we should. In my experience, I'm more fulfilled doing the things I choose to do. There's a sense of agency in my actions. Even if I don't succeed, I'm glad to have tried. In contrast, when I do things because it's the "default" next step, or when I follow advice I don't fully agree with, I lack the same resolve and motivation. At times I may even feel stuck.

Now I'm not telling you to only do the things you want or that which makes you happy. We all have obligations at work and at home. We cannot shirk our day-to-day responsibilities. But for major career and life decisions, the "default" choice—the safe choice, the choice of conventional wisdom—may not be the right choice for you. It comes down to this: Are you building the life you want, or are you building a life others want for you?

Take a moment to think about it. I had asked myself this question a few years ago. When I considered the various parts of my life—my career and finances, family and relationships, purpose and spirituality—the answer gravitated toward the latter more than I'd like to admit.

Perhaps you can relate. You may be tired of running the rat race and climbing the corporate ladder. Of faking smiles and going through the motions. Of keeping up with your peers or carrying the weight of your parents' dreams. Of building a life other people want for you.

The truth is that you will never please everyone. Some people will say you are too ambitious—or not ambitious enough. Others will say your decision is too risky, too rash, too this, or too that. They may be well-intentioned, and their advice may be sound. But they are not you. They don't know you and your priorities, your boundaries and your non-negotiables. If you don't either, you may be pulled every which way. You may find yourself heading down a path you never intended to take.

Many people today wrestle with questions of purpose. They followed the conventional advice. They went to college and earned their degree. They worked diligently and moved up. They added many letters after their name. Now they hold a respectable title and earn an enviable salary. Their colleagues admire them. Their friends applaud them. Their parents are proud of them. From the outside, it looks like they've made it. But they themselves aren't fulfilled. Can this be all there is to life?

I once heard a preacher on the radio talk about playing Monopoly when he was a child. He would buy and build and collect a lot of money. His parents and siblings just couldn't compete. He was in the zone. He was the master of the board. He felt large and in charge.

But a few hours later, it was time to put away the board, the tiny houses, the fake money. When all is said and done, none of it really mattered. He had nothing to show for his efforts. It was just a game. He compared this to our lives and challenged listeners to reflect: What will you have to show for your time on earth? Will you have made any lasting significance, or will it be like putting away a board game?

Life's too short to play meaningless games. To run around the board in a mindless frenzy. To chase fleeting pleasures and foolish goals. To accumulate wealth because society calls that success. Is this the life that *you* desire? After all, "there will come a day when you would give everything you have left to have what you have right now."[5] You don't want to regret how you had spent your best years.

"When the game is over, it all goes back in the box," writes John Ortberg. Everything will be put away, stored for future usage. And when your life is over, your toys will remain here, while you go into the box. That will be a reality for all of us one day. So while you can, you want to live well. You want to play the right game.

In the process, you want to "be the kind of player people want to sit next to."[6]

If you've taken the time to examine yourself—your values, passions, and priorities—you can walk in quiet confidence and renewed purpose. You can be intentional in your decisions and steadfast in your integrity. You can foster relationships that bring you the greatest peace and the deepest joy. You can find communities where you feel an undeniable sense of belonging. You can build the life you want.

Building a valuable network

We've talked at length about building individual connections and relating in community. But stepping back, you might ask: What makes a professional network valuable? I saved this question for the very end, because for all practical purposes, it shouldn't be your focus. Still, this may be useful to know. Here are the key traits that define a network.

- Network size: A larger network means that you have more people to help you. This includes not just those you know personally but also second-degree connections. As your network expands, your access to information tends to scale up. You'll hear of more opportunities, perhaps better ones, before your competitors. And when you have a question, you know more people to ask.
- Centrality: Consider not only the size of your network but the nature of the relationships. Is your network marked by tight clusters or loose ties? How central are you in these social circles? Are you in the core group or on the periphery? Do you bring people together like a hub-and-spoke, or are you part of existing cliques? Being central accelerates the velocity of information you get.

- Diversity: Most people have homogenous networks. They're surrounded by those who look and think like themselves. When possible, meet people from different backgrounds, life stages, and careers. Diversifying your network exposes you to new ideas and viewpoints. You can relate with more people. You can apply solutions from one sector to another. You can create real value.
- Depth of connections: While weak ties do have their place, stronger bonds tend to offer greater value. Think about the people you can rely on, the ones you can turn to in a pinch. They will support you when no one else does. They will do favors for you even at a cost to themselves. These relationships are not surface-level. They come from investment and reciprocity over time.
- Quality of contacts: Do you know excellent people? Do they embody a mindset of value? Are those in your network smart, capable, trustworthy, resourceful, well-connected, and influential? Such people have more to offer. Just as importantly, are you such a person? You cannot attract high-value people without providing value yourself. You must have something to offer them.

Keep in mind that these traits are not independent. They do affect one another. Network size is not the be-all and end-all. As you grow your network beyond a certain size, your quality of contacts may become diluted. You may fail to build deep connections. You may spread yourself too thin and lack the network centrality to be effective. Be careful not to optimize for one trait at the expense of the others.

There's another reason not to get fixated on this list. You may be tempted to plan and strategize and project-manage your network, while you should be out building relationships instead. Or you may start judging and scrutinizing people, instead of helping them with a cheerful heart.

As you consider the five elements, the tactics to employ and the habits to adopt, don't lose sight of the purpose. It's not about being "good at networking." It's about cultivating relationships, for which there is no one-size-fits-all approach, no scalable method or formula. The goal isn't to develop a massive network but the right network with the right people in it. When you do that, it will surely be valuable.

Thank you for reading. I hope that networking feels less mysterious or intimidating and more accessible to you. Like I shared at the beginning, I wanted to offer a common language for networking. Why? Because the words we use shape the way we think and drive the actions we take. Or as one author I met pithily articulates: "Books name realities."[7] Through this book, I hope to have accomplished just that.

The five elements framework centers us on the heart of networking. May we be credible and relatable people who consistently take initiative to create value for others. That is how we build meaningful connections and enduring friendships. That is how we all win.

Now go forth and do. Build the relationships, career, and life you want. Try different things. Lean into what works for you. Let the five elements of professional networking guide your path.

ACKNOWLEDGMENTS

The art of building relationships is not a matter of study but of application. Not of theory but of practice. You can't philosophize your way into understanding what makes people tick. You must go and interact with them. Through the feedback, possibly the friction, you learn what works and what doesn't. You reflect on your experiences and identify patterns. You carry those lessons into future situations.

Everything I know about networking I've learned from other people—from observing them, listening to them, and spending time with them. This book synthesizes and encapsulates those lessons. Friends regard me as a master networker. But the truth is: I've learned as much from them about relationships.

Here are the key individuals I would like to acknowledge. Most are still active in my life. Others had left an indelible impact in a prior season. I cherish all their friendships and the memories we've shared.

- Dennis Kulp, my best friend, a sterling individual—genuine and generous, loyal and true.
- Gina Lee, one of my dearest friends and confidantes. I'm so glad that we had reconnected.
- Ashley Radcliffe, a refreshing presence and caring friend. Your support means a lot to me.

- Jasmine Crouzet, who taught me patience and humility, lessons I had desperately needed.
- Kiet Ly, who modeled for me the importance of being adaptable and going with the flow.
- Vivian Jenner, who brings levity to any context. Her intellect is matched only by her humor.
- Aaron Byzak, a secular prophet, a trusted voice of reason in an increasingly unstable world.
- Chris Majdi, whose thirst for learning is insatiable, whose drive for growth is contagious.
- Bob Baker and Jordan Abel, warriors of faith, conduits of mercy to widows and the poor.
- Tom Dougherty and Victor Carrasco, who opened doors and demolished walls of doubt.
- Phil Brady and Clancey Stahr, who ushered me into the relational world of venture capital.
- Alan Sun and Elliott Siu, who spoke much-needed wisdom into my dating relationships.
- Anne Schuck and Lori Cardoza, without whom I wouldn't be half the writer I am today.
- Fawwaz Haq, Nick Carranza, and Chris Hernandez, who brought joy and meaning to work.
- Ray Gu, Aaron Brinkman, and Flora Vivanco—I couldn't have asked for better roommates.
- Travis Lindsay, my editor and friend, whose encouragement breathed life into this book.
- Rachel Thomas, whose wise counsel gave me confidence as I prepared for publication.
- Terry Whalin, Jill Nelson, and the rest of Morgan James Publishing, who believed in me.

- Christina Lee Smith, my sister and first friend in life. I know I can always count on you.
- Crystal Nguyen Nhu Thao, who saw in me that which I couldn't see in myself. You taught me more about relationships than anyone had before or since. May your memory live on.

I am grateful for these wonderful people God had placed in my life. Regardless of how we first met—whether by choice or by chance—we showed up for each other. Nobody succeeds alone. We all stand on the shoulders of giants, lifted up by fellow sojourners. They are our teachers and mentors, neighbors and friends. "As iron sharpens iron, so one person sharpens another" (Proverbs 27:17 NIV).

My wish is that you have people in your life who sharpen you. Who speak the truth to you in love. Who stand with you through good times and bad. Whom you can depend on and who also depend on you. May you find success in your work, fulfillment in your life, and joy in the company of friends.

ABOUT THE AUTHOR

C**hristopher K. Lee** is a healthcare and technology strategist. He has worked across the healthcare industry from a community clinic to an academic medical center, from a digital health startup to a Fortune 20 health insurer. Within these settings, he specialized in launching new products, programs, and services.

Chris is a venture partner at GoAhead Ventures, where he sources and evaluates early-stage technology startups. He teaches innovation at the UCLA Fielding School of Public Health, and he mentors founders for Techstars. He has also served as a participant ambassador for the NIH All of Us Research Program.

Outside of health and innovation, Chris is passionate about helping others find clarity for their lives and careers. He has spoken at dozens of universities and professional groups about work, meaning, and identity. He writes a newsletter on networking and career decisions at christopherklee.substack.com.

Chris graduated *summa cum laude* in psychology from UC Irvine and holds a Master of Public Health from San Diego State University. He has been quoted in *The Wall Street Journal, The*

Washington Post, Harvard Business Review, and *Forbes.* He lives in Orange County, California. In his leisure time, Chris enjoys swing dancing, writing music, taking nature walks, and exploring familiar places with fresh eyes.

REFERENCES

Preface
1. Horowitz, Ben. *The Hard Thing About Hard Things: Building a Business When There Are No Easy Answers.* New York: Harper Business, 2014.
2. Sarna, Surbhi. *Without a Doubt: How to Go from Underrated to Unbeatable.* New York: Simon & Schuster, 2023.
3. Cuddy, Amy. *Presence: Bringing Your Boldest Self to Your Biggest Challenges.* New York: Little, Brown and Company, 2015.

Introduction
1. Al Babbington, startup founder. Personal communication, 2014.
2. "Global Indicator: Employee Engagement," *Gallup.* https://www.gallup.com/394373/indicator-employee-engagement.aspx. Accessed August 1, 2024.
3. "Why People Quit Their Jobs," *Harvard Business Review,* September 2016. https://hbr.org/2016/09/why-people-quit-their-jobs. Accessed August 1, 2024.

Value
1. Carlson, Richard. *Don't Sweat the Small Stuff... and It's*

All Small Stuff: Simple Ways to Keep the Little Things from Taking Over Your Life. New York: Hachette Books, 1997.
2. Carnegie, Dale. *How to Win Friends and Influence People*. New York: Simon & Schuster, 1936.
3. Heath, Chip and Heath, Dan. *Made to Stick: Why Some Ideas Survive and Others Die*. New York: Random House, 2007.
4. Jun, Paul. "The Four Dirty C-Words of the Internet." *Paul Jun*, September 22, 2021. https://pauljun.me/the-four-dirty-c-words-of-the-internet. Accessed August 1, 2024.
5. Weldon, Glen. *NPR's Podcast Start Up Guide: Create, Launch, and Grow a Podcast on Any Budget*. Emeryville: Ten Speed Press, 2021.
6. DC Palter, angel investor. Personal communication, 2021.

Initiative

1. Nick Macchione, professor. Personal communication, 2014.
2. "The Pitch." *Seinfeld*, season 4, episode 3. NBC, 1992.
3. Prateek Sanjay, investor relations advisor. LinkedIn post, 2022.
4. Houpert, Charlie. "Charisma on Command." *YouTube*. https://www.youtube.com/@Charismaoncommand. Accessed August 1, 2024.
5. Cohen, Herb. *You Can Negotiate Anything*. New York: Bantam, 1982.
6. Yeung, Andrew. "How to Host an Industry Dinner." *Andrew Yeung*, January 31, 2024. https://www.andrew.today/p/how-to-host-an-industry-dinner. Accessed August 1, 2024.

Consistency

1. Pausch, Randy and Zaslow, Jeffrey. *The Last Lecture*. New

York: Hyperion, 2008.
2. "The Real Strength of Weak Ties," *Stanford Report*. September 15, 2022. Citing Erik Brynjolfsson. https://news.stanford.edu/stories/2022/09/real-strength-weak-ties. Accessed August 1, 2024.
3. Mara Rada, branding consultant. LinkedIn post, 2022.
4. Earley, Justin. *The Common Rule: Habits of Purpose for an Age of Distraction*. Downers Grove: InterVarsity Press, 2019.
5. *Always Be My Maybe*. Netflix, 2019.
6. Wyche, Keith and Booth, Renee. *Corner Office Rules: The 10 Realities of Executive Life*. West Chester: Kandelle Enterprises, 2013.

Relatability

1. Brooks, David. *How to Know a Person: The Art of Seeing Others Deeply and Being Deeply Seen*. New York: Random House, 2024.
2. Esenwein, Joseph Berg and Carnegie, Dale. *The Art of Public Speaking*. Springfield: Home Correspondence School, 1915.
3. "Axios Finish Line: Making a Friend," *Axios*. June 29. 2022. Citing Jeffrey Hall. https://www.axios.com/2022/06/30/how-to-make-friends. Accessed August 1, 2024.
4. White, John. *Daring to Draw Near: People in Prayer*. Downers Grove: InterVarsity Press, 1977.
5. Ferrazzi, Keith. *Never Eat Alone: And Other Secrets to Success, One Relationship at a Time*. New York: Crown Currency, 2014.
6. Greer, Peter; Horst, Chris and Haggard, Anna. *Mission Drift: The Unspoken Crisis Facing Leaders, Charities, and Churches*. Bloomington: Bethany House Publishers, 2014. Citing Albert Mohler.

7. Parry, Vince. *Identity Crisis: Health Care Branding's Hidden Problems and Proven Strategies to Solve Them.* New York: Parry Branding Group, 2016.

Credibility

1. Resnick, Nathan. "The Psychology of Social Proof." *HubSpot*, September 4, 2020. https://blog.hubspot.com/service/psychology-social-proof. Accessed August 1, 2024.
2. Gerald Bracht, hospital executive. Personal communication, 2013.
3. Anderson, David. "I Was Under Leveled! – Avoiding the Tragedy of Only Making $500k a Year." *ByteByteGo*, July 27, 2023. https://blog.bytebytego.com/p/i-was-under-leveled-avoiding-the. Accessed August 1, 2024.
4. Watts, Nigel. *Teach Yourself: Writing a Novel.* New York: McGraw-Hill, 1996.
5. "Purpose and Guidelines." *InterVarsity Blog.*
6. Andreessen, Marc. February 14, 2022. https://x.com/pmarca/status/1493458677553983488. Accessed August 1, 2024.
7. Burkus, David. *Friend of a Friend: Understanding the Hidden Networks That Can Transform Your Life and Career.* New York: Harper Business, 2018.

Conclusion

1. Chatterjee, Rhitu. "Why a Stranger's Hello Can Do More Than Just Brighten Your Day." *NPR*, August 23, 2023. https://www.npr.org/sections/goatsandsoda/2023/08/23/1193148718/why-a-strangers-hello-can-do-more-than-just-brighten-your-day. Accessed August 1, 2024.
2. Miller, Donald. *Blue Like Jazz: Nonreligious Thoughts on Christian Spirituality.* Nashville: Thomas Nelson Publish-

ers, 2003.
3. Anneliese Pixton, edtech founder. Personal communication, 2023.
4. "Sakura and Meiling's Friend." *Cardcaptor Sakura: Clear Card*, episode 16, NHK, 2018.
5. Chussil, Mark. "Don't Spend Your Life Making Up Your Mind." *Harvard Business Review*, May 15, 2017. https://hbr.org/2017/05/dont-spend-your-life-making-up-your-mind. Accessed August 1, 2024.
6. Ortberg, John. *When the Game Is Over, It All Goes Back in the Box*. Grand Rapids: Zondervan, 2009.
7. Albert Hsu, author and editor. Personal communication, 2024.

A free ebook edition is available with the purchase of this book.

To claim your free ebook edition:

1. Visit MorganJamesBOGO.com
2. Sign your name CLEARLY in the space
3. Complete the form and submit a photo of the entire copyright page
4. You or your friend can download the ebook to your preferred device

Morgan James BOGO™

A **FREE** ebook edition is available for you or a friend with the purchase of this print book.

CLEARLY SIGN YOUR NAME ABOVE

Instructions to claim your free ebook edition:
1. Visit MorganJamesBOGO.com
2. Sign your name CLEARLY in the space above
3. Complete the form and submit a photo of this entire page
4. You or your friend can download the ebook to your preferred device

Print & Digital Together Forever.

Snap a photo   Free ebook   Read anywhere

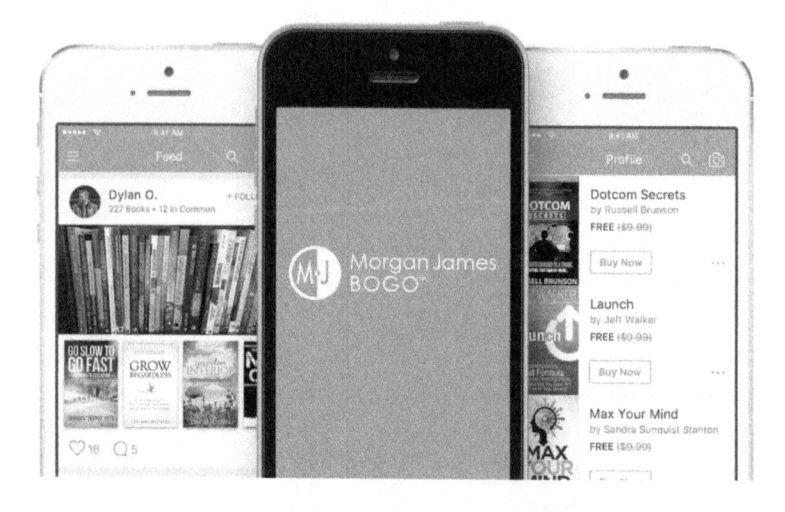